A WALK IN THE FOREST

A WALK IN THE FOREST

The Woodlands of North America

ALBERT LIST, JR.
ILKA LIST

ILLUSTRATED WITH PHOTOGRAPHS AND

DRAWINGS BY THE AUTHORS

Thomas Y. Crowell Company

New York

Library of Congress Cataloging in Publication Data
List, Albert, Jr. A walk in the forest.
Bibliography: p. Includes index. SUMMARY: Answers questions
about interacting areas of a forest. 1. Forest ecology—
Miscellanea—Juv. lit. 2. Forest ecology—North America—
Juv. lit. [1. Forest ecology—Miscellanea. 2. Ecology] I. List,
Ilka, joint author. II. Title.
QH541.5.F6L57   574.5'264   76-40171 ISBN 0-690-00990-9

1   2   3   4   5   6   7   8   9   10

To our parents,
Albert and Phyllis Carrington List,
who gave us our love of the woods

Contents

A WALK IN THE FOREST

1 The Forest

What is a forest?

A forest is a place where tall trees have stood for a long time, shading the ground below. It is a place where the leaves spread out in closely knit patterns against the sky, dividing it into tiny patches of blue and turning the light that passes through them green. Beneath this uppermost layer of the forest, the light is a cool green, except where shafts of sunlight drop down between the leaves, forming golden patches on the forest floor. When the wind shifts the leaves, the falling sunlight dapples the ground in changing patterns. Shorter trees, growing beneath those in the top layer, and still shorter shrubs shade the forest floor even more.

In many forests a great variety of plants grow beneath the trees. Ferns, mosses, and different kinds of flowering plants crowd all the available space. These plants grow in the soil and

A forest of towering tulip trees and dogwood and other small trees

rotting leaves, from the sides of fallen logs, and on rocks. While many plants crowd into the sunlight, others grow where the light is dim.

But not only plants make a forest. Animals that wiggle and creep, crawl and fly, live in the woods, too. There are animals that squeak, whistle, sing, and cry. There are animals that call or bark. There are animals that hop and climb and swim. There are animals that eat plants, and others that eat meat, and many that eat both. Some of these creatures live in the soil; others run among the ferns or spend their lives high up in trees. A few live inside of other animals—even inside of plants. You have heard of earthworms, slugs, toads, and frogs. You have probably seen chipmunks, mice, and squirrels. You have listened to the songs of warblers and chickadees. All these animals and many more live in the forest. The forest is a community of living things.

I have never been in a forest. What does it feel like?

A forest feels very different from a city or a town or even from a big field on a cloudy day. When you walk into a forest, you are suddenly shut away from the rest of the world. In summer the air in a forest is cooler and less dry than the air outside the forest. There is a leafy roof over your head, and under your feet the ground is soft. Your toes sink into it almost as if you were walking on a sponge.

You notice the air in a forest. It seems to have a shape, formed by the tall tree trunks growing close together. Tiny specks of dust drift in the golden streams of sunlight. The air curls under a fern frond and into the folds of a flower. It smells of leaf mold in one place, pine needles in another; here, some dusty ferns, and there, a mushroom that has been kicked over.

It is quiet in the forest, unless hundreds of birds are singing

Wood anemone

their early morning chorus, or the toads and frogs and crickets are calling their mates. The forest has the quiet of a place with a long history. If the trees are tall, they have been growing for fifty years or more. Generation after generation of animals has lived among them. The animals you find in the forest when you visit it are the descendants of animals that lived there hundreds of years ago, possibly thousands.

The forest in winter, unless it is an evergreen or coniferous forest, is no longer green and leafy, no longer such a private place. It is open to the sky because the branches of the trees are bare. And you can see quite a way into it, even from the road. The ground is frozen hard and perhaps covered with snow. The trees creak and groan in the wind, and all the animals are silent except perhaps for a cheerful group of chickadees.

Maple trees and white birches, leafless in the early morning mists of winter

What is a forest like in a rainstorm?

The leaves get wet and blow around, tossing and turning over in the wind. A few dead leaves and branches fall to the ground, torn off by the wind and the push of heavy rain. Sometimes bunches of green leaves are ripped off, too. In some storms lightning suddenly hits one of the trees and splits it right in half—from one end to the other. The inside of the ruined tree looks pale and splintered. Water runs over the leaves and drips off them onto the ground. It soaks into the dead leaves of the ground cover and runs down into the soil through every little hole. A few earthworms come struggling up out of the ground to get away from the water in their tunnels. If it rains hard enough and long enough, the tree trunks get soaking wet, and the moss and lichens growing on them turn bright green. This is because the green coloring in them shows through to the surface of the plants. You can see it better when the plants are wet and shiny.

White-breasted nuthatch

I went for a walk in the forest. I didn't see any animals. Where were they?

It takes a long time after you enter the forest to begin to see the animals. If you are very patient and stay still, and wait and watch and listen, animals that went into hiding when you first drew near will begin to go about their business again. The better you become at watching and waiting, the more you will see. The forest animals are busy finding food and eating it and building nests or tunnels or hideouts where they can live and grow and reproduce themselves.

The search for food is going on all around you in the forest. Birds move from branch to branch high in the trees or hop along the ground. They are looking for beetles, bugs, worms, moths, moth eggs, flies, seeds, fruits, and nuts. Squirrels and chipmunks run along the ground searching for grains, seeds, and nuts. If they find them, the squirrels will scurry off and perhaps go up a tree and out on a limb, while the chipmunks will dive into a small hole beneath a root or go into a crack between two rocks. Ants run along the ground close beside you, sometimes running over your hand or up your leg in a frantic hurry. Soon you may see the same ant coming back from its errand, dragging the body of an insect, huge by comparison. On a wet morning you may find a slug nibbling away at a leaf, or a snail in its shell napping for a spell during the hot part of the day. When a mosquito or a black fly lands on your arm to have its morning snack of blood, you may come to realize that the insects are the easiest animals in the forest to find and watch. The bigger animals stay out of sight if they possibly can. You may be able to watch squirrels and chipmunks, birds, turtles, and snakes, but you will have to be very lucky or do a lot of looking to see a deer, a raccoon, a shrew, or a skunk.

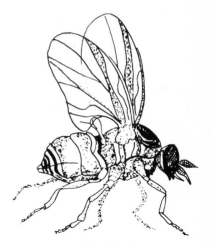

Blackfly

Are there different types of forests?

Yes, there are three main types of forests, but the two most commonly found in the Temperate Zone in North America are the deciduous forest and the coniferous forest. The deciduous forest is green only in spring and summer. In the fall its trees lose their leaves, The coniferous, or evergreen, forest is green the year around.

The third main type of forest is the tropical forest, which is also evergreen, consisting mostly of broad-leaved trees. There are small patches of semitropical forest in southern Florida.

What is the Temperate Zone?

The Temperate Zone is the part of the earth's surface lying between the Tropic of Cancer and the Arctic Circle in the Northern Hemisphere or between the Tropic of Capricorn and the Antarctic Circle in the Southern Hemisphere. The Temperate Zone has a warm summer season, a cold winter, and a spring and a fall when the temperatures are rather moderate. In North America the Temperate Zone extends from the southern United States—just beneath the tip of Florida—to northern Canada. Over most of this zone the temperature changes from hot in summer to cold in winter, but even these two extremes of temperature are moderate when compared to the bitter cold of regions above the Arctic Circle, or the extreme heat of regions below the Tropic of Cancer.

The flat, wide leaves of the red oak, a deciduous tree, and (opposite) some nearly ripe acorns from the same tree

How can I tell if I am in a deciduous forest?

If the trees above you have flat, wide, and rather soft leaves, the chances are that you are looking at the broadleaf trees in a deciduous forest. In such a forest the leaves sprout anew from the buds on young branches in early spring, and stay there until autumn when they all drop off, leaving the branches bare. Broadleaf trees flower when they are old enough, often not until they are twenty or more years old, and bear seeds that are protected inside fruits of various kinds—walnuts and acorns, for example.

How can I tell if I am in a coniferous forest?

If the trees above you have tough needle-shaped leaves and cones, you are probably in an evergreen forest. The leaves on coniferous trees may be long and slender like pine needles, short and pointed as in the spruce, or narrow and flat as in the hemlock. All evergreen leaves are weather-resistant: they can withstand extreme cold and heat. Conifers do shed their needles, but not all at once. The needles die and drop off a few at a time.

The cones may be up to twelve inches long as in the pine tree, about an inch long or a little less as in the hemlock, or still smaller and almost globe-shaped as in the white cedar, where the cones are no more than half an inch across. The cones are

A young balsam with its cones standing upright. This is the only coniferous tree whose cones remain upright at maturity.

brownish when ripe, and consist of tough, leathery scales arranged in a tight spiral. When the cones dry out, the scales separate, and the seeds flutter to the ground on thin, dry wings.

Are all broad-leaved trees in the Temperate Zone deciduous?

No, for in nature there are exceptions to every rule. The holly tree, for example, keeps its broad, tough, shiny leaves all year around, and is therefore an evergreen. The live oak, found in the southern part of the United States, also keeps its leaves all year around. In southern Florida most broad-leaved trees are evergreen.

Are all needle-leaved trees evergreen?

Again, most are, but not all. The larch or tamarack tree, for example, loses its needles in the fall. So does the bald cypress, which is found from southern Delaware to southern Florida.

Where do you find deciduous forests?

Temperate deciduous forests once covered eastern North America, from the Great Lakes region south to the Gulf of Mexico and west to the Mississippi River, beyond the Ozark Mountains. In 1600 these forests were mostly intact, except where Indian populations were large. As more and more settlers came from Europe, however, the forests were gradually destroyed by farming and logging. Although much has grown back, no more than one tenth of one percent of the original virgin forests remain.

Today some of the most beautiful deciduous forests are found in the New England states. There are deciduous forests, too, in

Larch

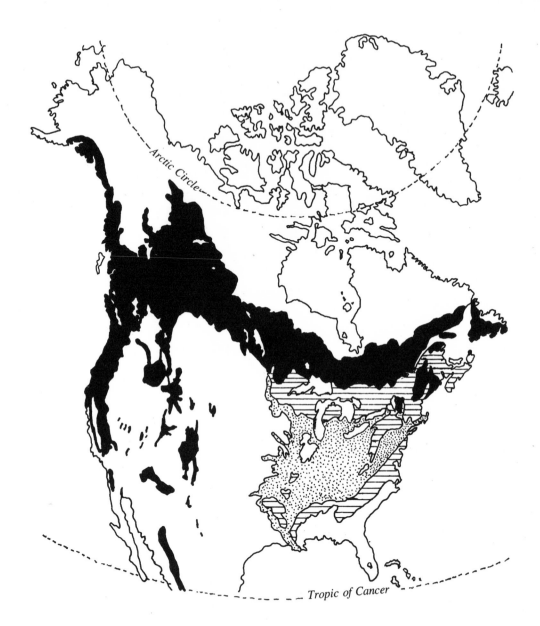

coniferous

mixed coniferous and deciduous

deciduous

North American forests

the area north of central Florida, east of the Great Plains, and south of the St. Lawrence River. There are also small patches of deciduous forest in the moist coniferous forests of the northwest, that extend from California to Alaska. These occur along river banks, where you find beautiful stands of western maple and red alder. All across Canada, too, you will find small deciduous forests along river banks and in burned-over or cutover areas.

Deciduous forests once covered most of Europe, the tip of South America, and parts of Japan and Australia. Here, too, only fragments of the original forests remain today.

Where do you find coniferous forests?

In the western regions of the United States you find broad bands of coniferous forests. These are part of the forested area that extends from Costa Rica in Central America north to the mouth of the Mackenzie River in Canada, west to the Brooks Range in Alaska, and east to Labrador. Across Canada the coniferous forest is anywhere from four hundred to eight hundred miles wide. Coniferous forests also grow in the eastern United States, down along the Appalachian mountaintops, from Mount Katahdin in Maine to the Great Smoky Mountains in North Carolina and Tennessee. They also extend across Russia in Siberia.

Do coniferous trees ever mix with deciduous trees?

Yes. Where the coniferous forests meet the deciduous forests in the northeastern United States—in Maine and New Hampshire, for example—you will find mixed coniferous-deciduous forests, with maple, beech, oak, pine, hemlock, balsam fir, and spruce trees growing together. And where the pine forests of Georgia and Florida meet the deciduous forests along the southern Appalachian Mountains, there is a mixed pine-oak forest—a rather extensive one at that. Places where two major communities meet and mingle are called ecotones.

You will also find coniferous trees, such as hemlock and pine, in groups or scattered here and there, in the middle of a deciduous forest. Some of the solid stands of pine that you see in New England are not part of the great coniferous forests of the north, but forests that have grown up in abandoned fields. You may see the stone walls that once bordered these fields running through the groves of pines. Young pine trees cannot get a start in full-grown broad-leaved forests, for they can grow only in bright light.

In Cornwall, Connecticut, there is a virgin stand of pine trees, called the Cathedral Pines, that are 150 feet tall. Underneath them grow hemlock, maple, and beech trees. If lightning knocks down one of the pines, or if a great tree dies and falls, some of these smaller, younger trees will grow taller and take the place of the virgin pines. In this way, such a forest gradually changes from a coniferous forest to a mixed deciduous, mostly beech-maple forest. Once it becomes a beech-maple forest, it will remain that way—unless a hurricane or fire destroys it—and we say it has reached its final—or climax—stage of development. Such a change, from one type of community to another, is called a succession. It is a word that describes how one group of living things replaces another.

Are there different kinds of deciduous forests?

Yes, there are, and each is given the name of the most important trees found in it. For example, in the northeastern United

The great coniferous forests of the North Cascade Mountains in Washington

States there are oak-hickory forests, maple-beech forests, and before the great American chestnut trees were wiped out by blight, there were also oak-chestnut forests. When two different kinds of trees are so often found together, we say they have formed an association.

In oak-hickory forests, the soil is dry. Often you find this association in places that have been burned over. These trees do not grow very large, and the forest is somewhat open. The trees are spaced out, and quite a bit of light reaches the ground. But no great variety of small plants grows there. Commonly you will find huckleberry, sheep laurel, and blueberry bushes in great abundance with perhaps a few small plants, such as wintergreen and pipsissewa.

Beech and maple trees, together with white, yellow, and black birches and elm and basswood trees, form many of the beautiful deciduous forests of the northeastern United States. In these, many different kinds of plants grow. Beneath the taller trees, you may find dogwood, wild black cherry, and hornbeam trees, as well as young maples, beeches, and birches. Closer to the ground you will find mountain laurel, hobblebush, viburnum, spicebush, Canada yew, and on the ground, mosses, ferns, fungi, and many kinds of small flowering plants.

Coniferous trees also form associations—for example, the spruce-fir forests of North America.

Why are there many different kinds of living things in some forests and not very many in others?

The amount and kind of plant and animal life that you find in a forest depends on how warm it is in the region, how much sunshine and rainfall the region gets, and what the soil is like. Where there is a large variety of living things, such as in moist deciduous forests, scientists say the forest has a high diversity.

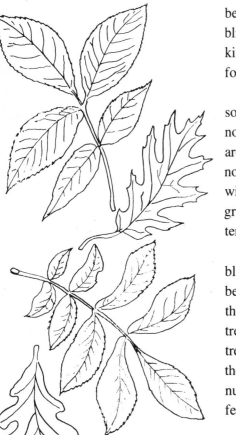

(Top to bottom) Shagbark-hickory, red-oak, pignut-hickory, and white-oak leaves

When not very many different kinds of things live in a forest, scientists say it has a low diversity.

The New Jersey Pine Barrens is an example of a forest with low diversity. It has a rather acid, very sandy soil with not much plant food in it. The main types of trees are pitch pine, post oak, and white cedar. The shrubs belong mostly to the heath family, whose members thrive in acid soil. Because there is too little calcium in the soil, earthworms and snails cannot live in the Pine Barrens. Without the proper amount of calcium, the earthworm cannot make its bristles nor the snail its shell.

Scientists believe that diversity is important. In a pure stand of trees, where there is low diversity, diseases can spread easily from tree to tree. In a mixed forest, with many different kinds of trees, disease can't spread as fast.

Can an orchard ever become a forest?

As long as an orchard is cared for by people who need its fruit, it will not become a forest. An orchard has a number of fruit trees planted in rows with measured stretches of open land between them. It takes a lot of energy to care for an orchard. People have to trim the branches and spray and fertilize the trees. When fruit trees are neglected, they begin to look wild. Their untrimmed branches become long and rangy, and lots of little branches, called suckers, sprout out all over the trees. If no one comes along to cut the grass in the open land between the rows, weeds and bushes begin to grow. Perhaps some acorns have been brought into the orchard, and perhaps a few pine seeds have spun through the air and landed there. If people stop caring for the orchard, these seeds will have time to grow. In twenty years the new growth might well be taller than the old fruit trees. Then these new trees will begin to shade the ground. The leaves they drop will change the soil beneath them. The

(Top to bottom) Sugar-maple and American-beech leaves

orchard grass will have died for lack of light, and small shade-loving plants will have begun to grow in its stead. After thirty or more years of neglect, an old orchard might begin to look and feel like a forest.

A forest is sometimes called an ecosystem. What is meant by that?

An ecosystem is a community of plants and animals including their physical environment. It can be as large as New York City or as small as a pool of water inside a woodpecker hole. Whether the community is large or small, the lives of all the animal and plant members are connected. All living things belong to an ecosystem.

What are the main parts of the forest community?

Ecologists who study plants and animals in the woodlands often divide the forest into four main layers. The uppermost layer is the *canopy,* which is sometimes as high as two hundred feet above the ground. It forms the leafy roof of the forest world. Beneath the canopy is the section known as the *middle layers*—the understory and shrub layer. Here stand the smaller trees and bushes. The *ground cover* includes all the small plants that live on the ground. It is the simplest part of the forest to study, for everything lies within easy reach.

Under your feet is the fourth main part of the forest—the *soil.* The soil is the place where most of the plants, from the tallest tree to the littlest moss, are anchored. It is crowded with bacteria, fungi, and animals that do the important job of recycling dead plant and animal matter, turning it back again into a form that can be used by the plants.

The four main layers of the forest

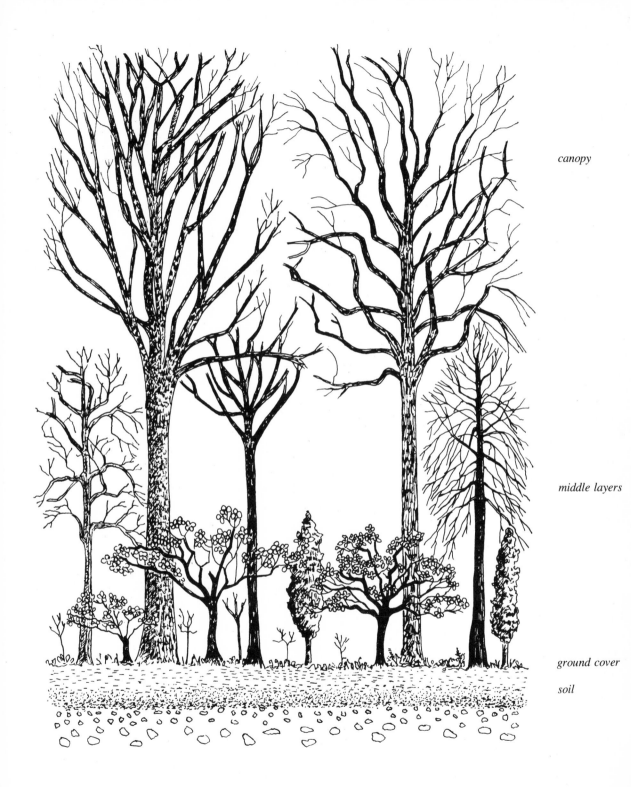

canopy

middle layers

ground cover

soil

Why do scientists talk about the forest in terms of layers?

Thinking of the forest as a community with four main layers is a natural thing to do, for each layer has distinct qualities. For example, each layer receives a different amount of light. Each has a different vertical location in space. And each section differs from the others in invisible ways, such as temperature and moisture—the soil and ground cover are wetter; the canopy is hotter and drier. But although the four main layers are different from one another, they are not separate communities. All are joined together through the cycling of matter and the flow of energy.

What are matter and energy?

They are the two most important things in all of life, that all living systems use and pass on from one to another. Matter is the stuff of which we are made, and energy—the capacity to do work—is what makes matter behave as a living substance. As living human beings, we constantly need many kinds of nutrient materials—minerals, such as iron; water; vitamins; fats; proteins; sugars; and starch—to build the matter we are made of. In plants mineral nutrients are taken in by the roots, and everything else is manufactured in the plants. Every plant makes its own vitamins, fats, proteins, sugars, starch, and so on. Animals get all their food from eating plants and eating each other. Nutrients flow through living things in the community in this way.

All living things need energy to make them "go." Plants capture the energy of sunlight with their molecules of chlorophyll and use the energy to turn carbon dioxide and water into sugars. Animals that eat plants get their energy from the sugars and starch stored in the leaves. Animals that eat other animals get their energy from them.

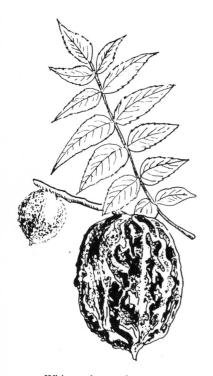

White walnut or butternut

When plants and animals in the woods die, the matter that each one is made of goes back into the soil. The energy is lost as heat into the air. Plant and animal matter are used over and over again as nutrients by new generations of living things. New energy flows endlessly from the sun into the forest, where it is trapped by the leaves.

What does it mean when you say that leaves trap sunlight?

The sun sends down a band of energy, to which man has applied several different names. Light is the kind of radiant energy we can see, but ultraviolet and infrared radiation also stream down. By means of pigments called chlorophyll, leaves capture perhaps as much as 2 percent of the light energy that reaches Earth. Chlorophyll is the stuff that makes leaves look green, and the easiest way to describe its complicated work is to say that chlorophyll serves as a kind of antenna tuned to receive the wave energy of light.

What does a leaf do with sunlight?

The chemicals in a leaf are arranged in a way that enables them to combine the energy of sunlight with carbon dioxide and water to make a food called glucose, a simple sugar. This process has the name of photosynthesis, which means a putting together by means of light. Water (H_2O) combined with carbon dioxide (CO_2) will make a glucose sugar ($C_6H_{12}O_6$), but *you* could not make sugar just by mixing these two ingredients and waiting for something to happen. If that were possible, you and I could just breathe on water, and we would get food. Only the light energy captured and changed to chemical energy by chlorophyll in the leaves has the power to put H_2O and CO_2 together

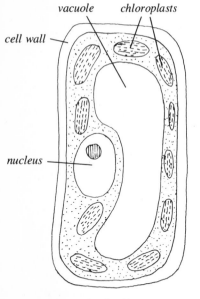

vacuole   chloroplasts

cell wall

nucleus

Leaf cell

and make glucose, along with some other sugars. Only plants can make chlorophyll with any degree of ease.

When leaves make glucose by photosynthesis, there is an ingredient left over. That vital substance, oxygen, is given off into the air—most of it, anyway. A part of it is kept for use by the leaves. The oxygen given off by green plants is the stuff that all animals must have to live. Not only do plants feed the world, but they also make most of the oxygen that we need to breathe.

The sun's energy is stored in the leaves in starch molecules until the tree needs to make use of it. Then part of the starch is turned back into sugar and carried in the sap throughout the tree. Some of it will be used as food, some in building the cellulose and lignin that make up the wood of the tree trunk and branches and the tough outer walls of cells, and some will be built into proteins in the living part of the cell known as cytoplasm. Through the food chain this energy is eventually divided into thousands of channels, as animals eat plants and other animals.

What is a food chain?

Plants and animals are linked together in an unbroken chain of eating habits. This means that the plants (the first link) make food that is eaten by animals (the second link) that need the food that the plants contain. The plant-eating animals in turn are eaten by other animals (the third link) that use them for food. In this way the food chain ties the lowliest and most ordinary of plants to the most complicated of animals. Many food chains start in the green leaves in the canopy of the forest.

Gypsy-moth caterpillars are one of the many kinds of insects that eat the leaves of trees. They get energy and nutrients from the leaves to build their bodies and keep their cells alive. As

Gypsy-moth caterpillar

they eat and use the food, they expend most of the energy that was stored in the leaf. They keep about 10 percent of it and store it in their growing or adult bodies.

If a bird makes a steady diet of gypsy-moth caterpillars, the bird will get the energy it needs from the flesh of the caterpillars. Most of this energy will be spent, too, in flying, breathing, eating, and for body heat, and about 10 percent will be used for growth of the body. From its diet of caterpillars a bird also gets the vitamins, minerals, and other chemicals it needs to build its body.

If the bird that lives on a diet of gypsy-moth caterpillars is itself eaten by a cat, a fox, or a hawk, its body will give food and energy to the animal that eats it. Again, some of the energy will be stored, but much of it will be used and lost as heat.

If the fox that ate the bird dies and begins to decay, small soil animals, bacteria, and fungi will get the nutrients and energy they need from the body of the fox. The river of energy from the sun gets thinner and weaker at this point, as it is divided again and again by smaller creatures. Eventually the last measure of energy is lost to the environment as heat. The invisible food chain has stretched from the top of the forest all the way down to the bottom.

A simple food chain

What would happen if our forests disappeared?

If you had been used to seeing forests all your life, you would probably be sad to see them disappear, for to you they are beautiful. Someone else who has always lived on open grassland or on the desert might not feel the same way. To him the forests might seem dark and scary places. The forests might also seem dark and forbidding to many city dwellers.

If forest land were to disappear, a number of things would happen. There would be changes in the climate over parts of the earth, as well as in the soil, the animal and plant life, and the water supply.

Forests tend to make the climate more moderate. This means that the daily changes of temperature over land having forests are not as great as in places without forests. During the day the leaves trap a good deal of the sunlight and give off large amounts of water. Thus, the air and the ground beneath the canopy is cooler and damper than it would be in an open field. At night the trees and living things of the forest give up some of their heat, but slowly so that the land does not cool off very rapidly. A desert, on the other hand, gets blistering hot during the day, for the sun falls directly on the ground and there is little if any evaporation of moisture, which keeps things cool. And at night the air and the ground become very cold, for there is little vegetation to retain the heat and slowly release it. The heat passes quickly away into the sky.

Trees also affect the supply of water, and that is why usually forest lands are kept around reservoirs. When it rains in the forest, the water is absorbed and held in the spongy humus of the forest floor and released only slowly. In a desert the water either runs off in violent floods or else evaporates as soon as it hits the ground. A land that is heavily forested usually has a better water supply.

If there were fewer forests, there would also be less wood, and people would have to find other materials to use instead.

Of course, forests are the homes of an enormous variety of living creatures, and if all the trees were to disappear, there would be fewer places for these organisms to live. When you enter the woods, you can see at a glance that there are hundreds of different kinds of plants living there, and only a little more hidden are thousands of different kinds of animals.

2　The Canopy

What is the canopy?

The canopy is the roof of leaves made by the tops of the tallest trees in the forest. It forms a barrier between the bright hot sky and the forest below. In some forests the canopy is a hundred to two hundred feet above the ground; in others it may be no more than twenty-five. Its height depends on the kinds of trees in the forest. When you explore a forest, it is a wonderful thing to sit for a while, and leaning all the way back, watch the patterns and movements of the leaves in the canopy.

Because their topmost leaves lie in the brightest light, the trees that reach into the canopy are able to make and store more food than the other trees and plants in the forest. Their great height and huge trunks show how much food they have produced. Thousands of insects live in the canopy and eat the leaves. Many birds live there, too, building their nests a little below the

Looking up into a canopy formed by white oaks

highest boughs, where they are sheltered from storms and the most intense rays of sunlight.

The canopy is important in another way, too. It adds most of the litter—the dead leaves, branches, seeds, and so on—to the forest floor. As these begin to decay, they serve as food for millions of soil animals, and add humus to the soil. The humus makes the soil rich in the nutrients all plants need for growth and increases the water-holding capacity of the land.

How can you see what is going on in the canopy?

From the forest floor it is hard to see what is happening in the canopy. The only way you can really observe it closely is to go up there and stay a while. Biologists who want to study animals in the canopy or lichens on the high tree branches sometimes build platforms in the canopy. They add swing-out seats, so they can get away out under the branches. That is certainly one way of doing it, but few people ever have this kind of opportunity. The next best thing is to use binoculars or simply to listen to the sounds of birds and insects coming from the treetops.

A beautifully patterned canopy of walnut trees

But there is another way as well, and that is to study the things that fall from the canopy to the forest floor. Branches and leaves drop from the trees. Dead branches fall, and so do live branches after storms or high winds. Some of these branches will have flowers or seeds on them. Some of the leaves that fall will show signs of having been eaten, or they will have on them strange swellings or soft cocoons. On a leaf you may find an insect that doesn't seem to realize it is now living on the ground.

Because it is so hard to get into the canopy, you will have to become a detective and study it from a distance, relying on whatever evidence you can find.

Why is there so much green?

There is so much green because every leaf in the canopy contains the chlorophyll pigments. When you look up at the leaves of the canopy, the green is the first thing you notice. All the leaves, no matter what their shape, whether they are broad or narrow, long or short, seem to be colored one shade of green or another. Yet while most leaves are green, not all are. Sometimes another pigment hides the green chlorophyll that is present in all leaves. That other pigment is red in the copper-beech tree and in the leaves of some other trees and plants you may find.

Is chlorophyll found in every part of a leaf?

To get an idea of where the chlorophyll is, it is best to try to understand how a leaf is put together. Pictures of how a leaf looks under a microscope will show you parts you are unable to see with your eyes alone.

The leaf of a tree, like every other leaf, consists of thousands of cells, the tiny building blocks of which almost all organisms are made. There are many different kinds of cells in a leaf, and they are arranged in a certain way.

Wax-coated cells, called epidermal cells, form the outside layer or skin of the leaf. Next in broadleaf trees, such as the oak and maple, come a couple of palisade layers. The palisade cells are the main light-capturing cells, and they are full of chloroplasts, which are small containers that hold the chlorophyll. Farther into the leaf are cells that make the veins and give the leaf its strength. Alongside the vein cells are spongy cells where air spaces are. The veins themselves are like an elegant plumbing system in a very busy chemical factory. They supply every part of the leaf with water and chemicals, just when and where they are needed. On the bottom of the leaf is the lower skin, or epidermis, made of more epidermal cells. It is usually filled

Cross section of a deciduous leaf

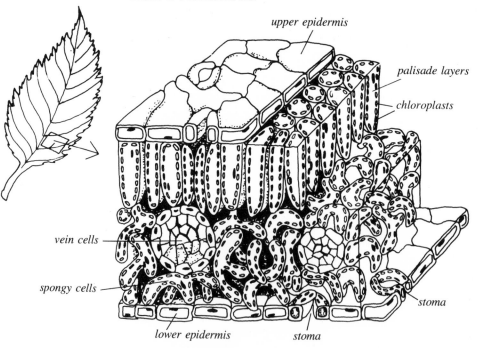

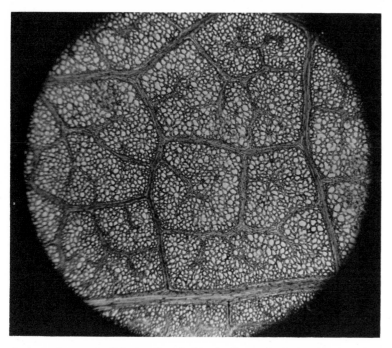

A photomicrograph of the interior of a bit of tulip-tree leaf, showing the veins (dark) and the air spaces (light)

with little holes. Each hole is called a stoma, or mouth, and is controlled by a pair of guard cells that can open or close it. Air passes in and water vapor out through the stomata.

Some leaves have other kinds of cells—hair cells, stinging cells, oil cells, water cells, milk cells, and so on.

Are the needles on coniferous trees really leaves?

Yes, they are leaves. Although their shape is very different from the flat, wide, rather soft leaves on deciduous trees, needles are like other leaves in many ways. They have the same chlorophyll, chloroplasts, spongy cells, and stomata. Because of the needlelike shape, however, the arrangement of cells is a little different from the arrangement of leaves on a broadleaf

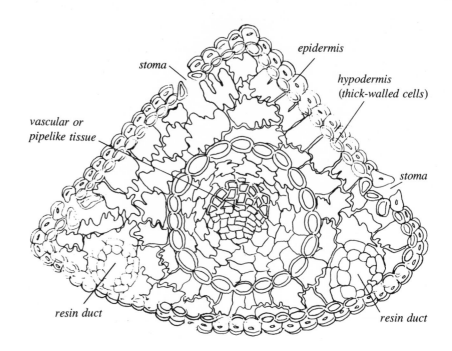

stoma

epidermis

hypodermis
(thick-walled cells)

vascular or
pipelike tissue

stoma

resin duct

resin duct

Cross section of a needle

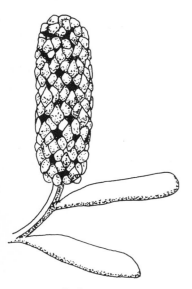

Podocarpus

tree. The stomata are placed in rows, running down the whole length of the needle, for example. In the middle of the needle, also running down its whole length, is a rod or two of pipelike tissue, veins through which food and water move in and out of the leaf, coming and going from other parts of the tree. A conifer needle has a tough layer of thick-walled cells just under the epidermis that makes it strong enough to stand winter winds without tearing and helps to keep it from drying out. The sticky resins that you often feel when you touch the bark of a coniferous tree are also found in the needles.

Were needles ever like other leaves?

It seems likely that long ago conifers had wider, flatter

leaves. *Cordaites* is the name of a conifer that lived 250 million years ago. Its fossils show that the tree had a wide, flat leaf. Scientists believe that in the course of evolution the shape of the leaves on conifers may have changed to the narrow, sharply pointed shape that we now know. There are still some conifers, growing in other countries, that have wider leaves: *Araucaria*— the Norfolk Island pine—and *Podocarpus* are examples.

Some leaves have taken quite the reverse course of evolution. For example, the ancestors of the ginkgo tree had fan-shaped leaves with much-divided parts, but now the ginkgo's leaves are solid with either one or two lobes on the blade.

Ginkgo

What makes needles and other leaves a certain shape?

While all leaves start out alike as little bumps on the dome of tissue at the tip of a branch, they also all end up with the shape characteristic of their species. The shape of leaves is inherited, just as the color of your hair or the shape of your face is inherited. But while all the leaves on a maple tree, for example, look alike, if you examine them closely and really compare them, you will find that each leaf is just a little different. Some are bigger than others; some are smaller; some are crooked in one place or another. One very common tree—the sassafras—has leaves with three different shapes, but that is very unusual. On most trees the shape of the leaves is pretty much alike. The development of shape in plants and animals is still one of the profound mysteries of biological science.

What are the lines on a leaf?

They are patterns made by the veins, or vascular bundles as they are also called. You don't notice the veins on a needle, but

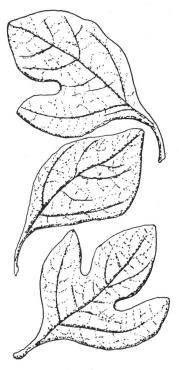

Sassafras

on the leaf of a deciduous tree, they are often quite apparent.

Each kind of leaf has its own vein pattern. In many cases, you can see some of that pattern just by looking at the leaf. You will see more of it if you hold the leaf up to the light, and still more if you are lucky enough to have a microscope. The veins are like plant fingerprints.

Veins, with their thick vessel walls, help to strengthen the soft tissue of the leaf and hold its flat form out to catch the light—just as the ribs of an open umbrella support the soft cloth that catches the rain. But the veins of a leaf are more important than the ribs of an umbrella. Veins carry water to every cell of the leaf.

Typical vein patterns

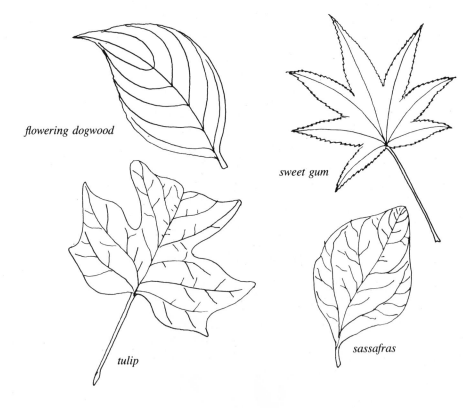

flowering dogwood

sweet gum

tulip

sassafras

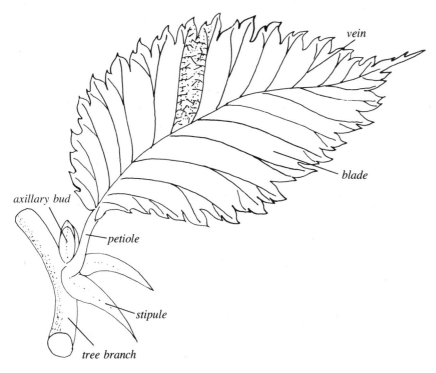

A typical deciduous leaf

Why does a leaf have a tough stalk?

A leaf has a tough stalk so that come what may—strong winds, ferocious rainstorms—it will not fall off the tree. Often after a bad storm you will find on the ground a whole group of leaves still attached to a twig. The inflexible twig was snapped off in the wind, but the leaves remained where they belonged.

The stalk of a leaf is tough and flexible. It is called a petiole. It can twist and turn a great deal without breaking or crushing, so that even in a storm water and food can move in and out of the leaf through its stem.

The leaves of coniferous trees are firmly attached to the twig right at the base of the needles, so they don't have stems in the same sense that the leaves on broadleaf trees have them.

How does a leaf stick on a tree?

Many leaves stick on trees at the base of their stalks by a flexible region of cells called the pulvinus. In the pulvinus there are no stiff fibers as there are in the rest of the stalk. Instead there are fat little cells full of water.

To us it looks as though a leaf is motionless unless the wind blows, but this is not true. The pulvinus is like a motor that can cause the whole leaf to move slowly. A leaf can change its angle and move up or drop down, sticking out from its stem in different directions at different times of the day, and move with a regular rhythm.

Why do leaves sometimes droop?

When a tree or other plant needs water, its leaves begin to droop. If it rains or you give it water, its leaves soon perk up and recover their stiffness. If you break a leaf off a tree, the same thing happens. It begins to droop. That is because it is no longer getting water from the tree's roots. The stiffness of the cells of a leaf is called turgor by plant physiologists. Turgor pressure is what holds a leaf up. The water pressure inside the cells is often higher than the air pressure inside a bicycle tire. You can get an idea of what water pressure can do by filling a balloon at a faucet. When the balloon is full, it is firm; when you let out a lot of the water, it becomes floppy.

You cannot see a plant drink water. But if you take a piece of celery and put it in some water colored with food dye, you can see color move up the stalk with the water. Water moves up the trunk of the tree in the same way.

How it happens can be explained as follows. A plant cannot keep water in its leaves because of the tiny holes, or stomata, in them. Water is always going out of the leaf into the air. Soon there is too little water in the leaf. As long as the leaf is attached to the plant, this is no problem, for more water is brought up to it from below. The roots are always collecting water from the soil. But if the leaf has been broken off the tree or plant, it loses water which it can't replace.

You can see this very clearly if you pick a leaf from a broad-leaved tree. When you pick a conifer needle, however, it doesn't wilt because it is so much stiffer. It still loses water, but more slowly.

Why do the leaves on broadleaf trees turn red, orange, and yellow in the fall? Why do they turn brown?

In the spring and summer the chlorophyll pigments are in high enough concentration to hide the yellow and orange pigments in the leaves. These pigments are always present. When the fall comes, with its cold nights and bright warm days, the chlorophyll in the leaves on some trees changes and finally disappears, and the yellow and orange pigments begin to show.

As the cold nights and bright warm days continue, other trees, such as oaks and maples, that have not yet lost their chlorophyll and are still making sugar, change some of the sugar into bright red pigments. Then as the chlorophyll fades, the bright red pigments in the leaves splash the forest here and there with their own brilliant color.

After a time, when the frosts begin to get heavy, the bright colors gradually disappear, and the leaves start dropping to the ground and turning brown. The brown color is caused by yet another kind of pigment called tannin. It, too, is formed from substances that were already present in the leaves. The leaves that still cling to some trees, such as oak trees, also turn brown. As the leaves on the ground get wet from rain and pack down,

they darken even more and begin to rot. After a time, as much as several years later, they turn black and become part of the soil.

Why do conifers stay green all year around?

They stay green because their needles are alive all year around. The leaves on deciduous trees die in autumn, but pine needles and hemlock needles, spruce and fir needles, stay alive for several years and never all die at the same time. New needles are made each spring, and throughout the year some of the older needles drop off. This change is not very noticeable on a conifer, but you can tell it's happening by the new layer of brown needles on the ground underneath the tree each year.

Needles can withstand a lot of cold and ice and snow. They can freeze quite solid without being harmed. Even though needles look tough, they are very sensitive to air pollution. The poisons in the air collect in them little by little, and when too much pollutant has gathered, the tips begin to die and turn brown. Finally, whole needles may fall off the tree prematurely.

Why do leaves, twigs, and flowers appear on broadleaf trees in the spring? Why not in the fall?

In the spring, when the days are no longer so cold and the ground is growing mushy as it defrosts, the substance called sap begins to move up through the tree trunk. It comes from the roots where it was stored and flows through all the branches into the tiniest twigs. It moves into the winter buds that are along the sides and at the ends of these twigs. The sap contains sugar and other substances that the buds need in order to grow. The sap starts the buds growing in the spring because only then do they receive the hormone message that says *grow*.

Looking up at the canopy in a dense stand of white pine

The sap starts moving because trees, and other plants as well, have something inside them that scientists call a biological clock. It is a way that all plants have of measuring what time of day and what time of year it is. Using hormones as messengers, the clock tells the plant when it is time to put out leaves, when it is time to flower, when it is time for the leaves to fall, as well as other things.

You wouldn't be able to take a plant apart and find such a clock, for it has no known shape and doesn't run on electricity or by a spring. It is thought to be a biochemical clock made of molecules. These molecules respond to changes in the environment, such as the shifting in the temperature, the length of the daylight, and the amount of moisture. Depending on how its molecules respond, a plant knows what to do and when to do it.

Biological clocks are known to exist in algae, insects, birds, and practically every living organism, including people. People have at least twenty things they are likely to want to do every

Two stages in the swelling and opening of buds on a Norway-maple tree. In the first photograph, the buds have just begun to open. In the second, taken a few days later, the leaves have already emerged.

day at certain times because of their biological clocks. These things could be called activity rhythms and include eating, sleeping, waking, working, and playing.

If plants did not have a biological clock, they would open their buds at any time of year when it became warm enough for the buds to grow. Because trees and other plants have ways of measuring the periods of darkness each day, the buds open only in the right season when there is usually plenty of moisture in the soil and when, day after day, the weather is warm.

Norway maple

Where do baby broadleaf trees come from?

Baby broadleaf trees come from fertilized eggs. Many trees have flowers of two kinds: male and female. Some of these flowers are so small you can hardly see them. Others such as those on the tulip tree are large and very beautiful.

The pollen grains from the male flowers drift through the air to the female flowers. When a sperm from a male pollen grain unites with an egg in a female flower, the fertilized egg begins to grow into a baby tree. At this time the young plant is called an embryo, and it is protected inside a seed. The embryo of the birch tree becomes a plant smaller than a pinhead inside the tiny birch seed. An acorn is also a seed, and the embryo that lies within it changes into a complete plant while the seed waits for the proper time to grow. When the seed sprouts, the tiny plant that emerges already has a root and a shoot with several leaves.

Do maple trees have flowers?

Yes, there are many kinds of maple trees, and like all broadleaf trees, each kind has flowers. Maples are among the first of the trees to bloom. In the early spring the red maple flowers first, and the sugar maple follows soon after. The flowers of the red maple are red. Those of the sugar maple are yellowish green. The fertilized female flowers of the sugar maple eventually develop into winged fruits called samaras. Other maple trees make samaras, but they are not as large as those on the sugar maple. The wings of the samaras act as propellers, and whirl the fruits through the air. Sometimes they fly quite a distance. Each half of the double samara carries one maple seed in its thick end. Chipmunks and other animals love these seeds and strip them from the inside of the fruit and store them. In fact, the seeds of such trees as the maple, oak, and dogwood are very important sources of food for woodland animals.

Most tree flowers live only a few days, but some of the fruits that develop cling to the trees until late in the winter, as those of the birch tree do.

As the old saying goes, Great oaks from little acorns grow. How?

Acorns usually drop from trees in the fall and lie on the ground over the winter. Lots of them are eaten by animals. But some of them are left, and in the wet spring they come to life.

The first thing to pop out of an acorn when it germinates or sprouts is the primary root. It is called the radicle. Next comes the shoot and a few small leaves. The seed leaves of an acorn, called the cotyledons, stay inside the seed coat. They are filled with much food—starch and some protein and fatty substances. The growing seedling uses this food for many months. But as the little plant begins to do well on its own, the seed leaves shrivel up. The young oak has grown slowly so far, but now it begins to shoot up fast.

The familiar cap of the acorn is a small bed of tiny leaves in

Sugar-maple (top) and
Norway-maple flowers

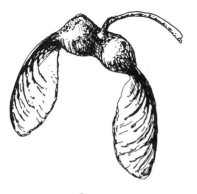

Samara

which the nut develops. When the acorn germinates, the cap falls off and begins to decay.

An acorn can *start* to grow anywhere it happens to land if that spot has a little bit of moisture, some soil, and some light. But while the acorn can start to grow anywhere, it may not be able to keep on growing. That depends on whether its root can find enough moisture and nourishment in the soil and on whether the shoot can make its way into the sunlight.

Some seeds cannot grow where they land. For example, if the tiny seeds of certain trees land in even a slightly bad place—for them—they die soon after they sprout. The bulky acorn has plenty of food stored in it to give it a good start, but small seeds are more delicate and have no reserves of energy and moisture.

One day in early spring I saw a great cloud of golden powder blowing out of a conifer. What was it?

That was a cloud of pollen being swept out of the male cones by the wind.

Why does a pine tree have pine cones?

We often find pine cones lying on the ground, but they began their life up among the needles of the pine tree. It is in the cones that the seeds are born which will one day flutter to the ground and create new trees.

Each year a new set of cones opens on the tall pines. Like the needles, they were formed in the buds the year before. The little green cones stand upright on the branches. They are very small, just a little more than an inch long. On a female cone, the scales that wind around it in the spiral that makes up most of the cone separate just long enough to catch the pollen grains, flying like

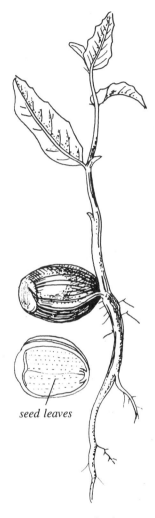

seed leaves

Acorn germinating

Young, rapidly growing needles of the slash pine in Florida and very young, green cones on a white-pine tree, their scales still tightly closed

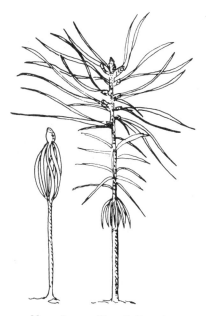

New pine seedling (left) and same seedling two years later

dust specks in the air. The pollen grains bring male sperm cells to the female egg cells waiting inside the seeds of the cone. If pollen did not come to the cone, no pine embryos or seeds would be formed.

If it seems funny for a tree to have eggs, remember that they are not like birds' eggs with a yolk and a great deal of white. They have proteins, but no yolk or white at all. Though they are as large as most plant eggs, they are so small they can be seen only with a microscope.

When the seeds are ready to grow, the cone scales change from green to light brown, and the cones hang down. The cones dry out and open. From beneath the prickly scales, the seeds flutter out. Sometimes most of the seeds on a tree are eaten by red squirrels before they are even ripe. Many other seeds die, but some always are left to become like little seedling pines.

ANIMALS IN THE CANOPY

What is the name of the worm that stood as still and as straight as a stick when I bothered it?

You must have found an inchworm, or looper, that has dropped to the forest floor. Its family name, *Geometridae*, means to measure the earth, but the inchworm properly belongs up in the canopy, munching away at the leaves of elm, oak, hickory, and maple trees. Although inchworms are not very big, they have a grand appetite, and enough of them feasting together can strip a tree of its leaves. As plant eaters, inchworms are a first link in the food chain that leads to higher animals. Many of the inchworms provide food for birds.

When they are startled, inchworms stand erect and look like twigs. They have legs only at the ends of their bodies. When they are in motion, they form loops from end to end and look as if they were measuring whatever surface they are walking upon. Some kinds of inchworms roll up tubes of leaves and tie them together with silk, making cocoons inside of which they will change into moths.

What kind of animal is it that eats a leaf down to its veins?

The larval stages of butterflies, moths, and sawflies—that is, during the period or phase when the young insects are like worms in shape—all go to work on leaves, each kind of larvae enjoying certain parts. If a leaf is eaten down so that only its veins are left, we say that it has been eaten by a leaf skeletonizer. Some larvae eat up both leaves and veins, while others eat only what lies between the tougher parts. Some tiny larvae live inside the leaf itself, eating the soft tissue.

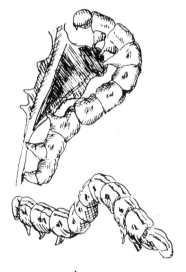

Inchworms

A leaf of the witch hazel, rolled up by an insect larva

What causes those twisty-turny patterns you sometimes see on leaves?

Those patterns are actually tunnels made by various leaf-miner insects in their larval stage. They use the inside of the leaf as a source of energy. Each different kind of leaf miner makes a different-looking tunnel between the upper and lower epidermis of the leaf. It does this by eating and chewing the inside of the leaf away. The larvae are very small and flat, as they would have to be to fit within the leaf. The tunnels show up on the outside of the leaf as grayish and white patches.

Do leaf-eating insects eat any leaf they find?

Some insects are very choosy about what they eat, and some are not. A silkworm will eat only mulberry leaves, and it dies of starvation without them. But the Japanese beetle eats about 250 different kinds of leaves, and the caterpillar of the gypsy moth finds about 400 kinds to its liking. That makes the gypsy-moth caterpillar the enemy of nearly every deciduous tree in the woods.

I found a little, round tan-colored ball the size of a golf ball on the forest floor. What was it?

You must have found something called a leaf gall, shaped out of a red-oak leaf by a tiny, black wasp larva. Galls are growths, or swellings, and they can be made on leaves, the stems of plants, seed pods, and even branches or twigs. Although many, many kinds of leaves may have one kind or another of gall on

Galls on red-oak tree

them, the galls are rarely numerous enough to interfere with photosynthesis.

Some galls are very small; some are large. Some are black or dull colored; some are bright, even red or orange. Some are hard and tough; some soft and fragile. Galls can be caused by many organisms besides wasp larvae—fungi, bacteria, mites, and nematodes. Each makes a gall with a particular kind of shape.

The larva that makes the red-oak leaf gall hatches from an egg laid by the tiny mother wasp just below the surface of the leaf. The small larva begins to eat the leaf, and as it does so, its saliva begins to affect the plant tissue of the leaf. It makes the leaf grow into a hollow ball with complicated patterns of cells inside. When the larva becomes an adult it leaves the gall by drilling a tiny hole through the wall of its "house."

What is the insect that calls in the night, "Katy did, she didn't, she did!"?

That is the katydid, who calls its own name over and over into the night. The noise is made by a triangular part on the upper side of the wings that has little pickets and scrapers on it. When these are rubbed together, they make the call.

The songs are the courtship calls made by the male katydids to attract females. If you want to know how hot the summer night is, count the number of calls made every minute, add 161° F. to it, and divide the total by 3. This works because the temperature affects how many times per minute the katydid makes its sound.

The katydid looks so much like the leaves that it lives among high in the canopy that you have to be very close to the insect before you can see it.

Katydid

I heard a buzzing sound coming from the treetops. What was it?

That was the sound of male cicadas—sometimes called locusts—announcing that they are ready to mate. Male cicadas keep up the racket until they have attracted females. Soon after the males and females mate, the males die and drop to the ground. The females stay in the branches for a few more days and lay their eggs in the bark of twigs. Then they, too, die and drop to the ground. The insects that hatch from the eggs do not look very much like the parents. They suck the juices from the twigs in the canopy for a while. Then they drop to the ground and begin to dig themselves in. They are going to stay there for a long time. While underground, they suck the juices from tree roots.

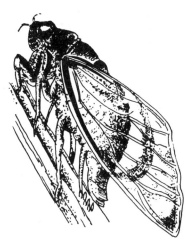

Cicada

Different kinds of cicadas spend differing lengths of time underground—as little as one year or as much as seventeen years. When they have finished growing and changing, they crawl out of the ground and climb up into the canopy. The males buzz loudly as they call for mates, and the cycle starts over again.

From the moment the cicadas leave the ground, a good number of animals prey upon them for food: hawks and other birds, and even turtles and skunks. Some years only a few cicadas emerge, but other years they appear in huge numbers, making roads and sidewalks slippery with their crushed bodies. Their strange appearance and their great numbers can be frightening, but they are harmless to people. And usually they do not damage the trees very seriously.

I saw a sudden flash of bright red high up in the canopy. What could it have been?

If you live in the northeastern part of the United States, the

Scarlet tanager

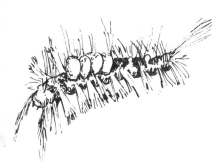

Tussocked caterpillar

Leafhopper

chances are that you saw a scarlet tanager, a bird that is not easy to spot among the thick leaves of the summer canopy. Sometimes in the spring you will see one perched on a branch, pecking away at the new leaves. But it is not eating the small green sprouts. It is eating the tiny newborn caterpillars on them.

There are a great many birds that hunt insects in the canopy—several kinds of warblers and the yellow-throated vireo, among many others. In fact, wherever there are insects, there are birds. The scarlet tanager is one of the brightest. It hops around finding plain caterpillars, tent caterpillars, tussocked caterpillars, inchworms, leafhoppers, mites and worms, moths, flies, and beetles.

Birds are very important in the forest, because most of them live on a diet of insects. They form the third link in the food chain. Only certain birds—the *raptors,* a group that includes hawks and owls—eat the flesh of higher animals, such as mice. Even birds that eat grain as adults are fed insects by their parents while they are still in the nest. But most of the birds in the forest eat mainly insects.

The number of insects in the world is always huge, and at least 50 percent of all insects eat plants. Leaves in the canopy, leaves everywhere, make excellent food for insects, and every year a tree puts out at least as many leaves as the year before, and probably a lot more. Insects can depend on a huge supply of food being handy for them. Through evolution they and other plant eaters—nematodes, fungi, and mites, for example—have developed forms that feed off leaves in every imaginable way. Never are there so many of these vegetarians that they eat up all the leaves though! One reason is that birds live in every part of the forest, working hard to find insect food. Many insects also eat other insects, but birds are more important in controlling the insect population because they eat more of them.

I saw a sort of sack hanging from the end of a branch. How did it get there?

Two different kinds of hanging sacks are made by common birds. They are both nests. One of them is made by a bird called the Baltimore oriole from twigs and plant fibers that are shaped into loops and tied together. It hangs from the thin end of an elm branch in the canopy, out too far for any animal such as a cat or squirrel to go. Another hanging nest is made by the red-eyed vireo and slung from the fork of a branch in the middle layers. It is not as high up or as far out on the limb as the nest of the oriole. The vireo's nest is made of bark, paper, and plant down, with bits of cocoon mixed in.

Where do most birds nest?

Most build their nests near their food supply. Depending on the kind of bird, the nest is built in a certain way, in a certain kind of place. A few birds nest high in the canopy; and a number, on the ground; but most nest in the middle layers of the forest—anywhere from two to forty feet up. Some warblers build in the canopy, and find their insect food among the upper leaves. Woodpeckers nest in the middle layers in hollowed-out tree trunks, and find their food in the bark. A few birds, such as the ovenbird, the hermit thrush, and the black-and-white warbler, build in hidden spots on the ground.

What was the big pile of sticks I saw at the top of a tree?

It is bound to have been a nest, and if you return and watch it carefully, you may be able to find out who lives there. It could have been built by a squirrel, a crow, or a red-tailed hawk for all these animals build nests of sticks.

Baltimore oriole

Ovenbird

Red-tailed hawk

When does a hawk hunt?

A hawk hunts during the day. It has wonderfully keen eyesight, and as it rides the air currents high above the fields, it watches the ground below for certain signs of movement. A hawk can spot mice, chipmunks, rabbits, and other small rodents from great heights. It can dive down so quickly that it can catch an animal before it has a chance to disappear into a hole. Most hawks eat insects, frogs, snakes, and sometimes birds, as well as rodents. Many hawks nest high in the canopy in the forest, and when they have caught something, they often return there to share the food with their young.

How do owls find their food in the dark?

Owls have eyes that focus very quickly on things at different distances. They see very clearly in three dimensions because they have what is known as binocular vision, as we do. Although owls can see in the daytime, they can also see in very little light. If there is no light at all, they depend on their ears to guide them. One ear faces up and the other faces down, and owls can tell exactly where something is by turning their heads and listening. Their heads are set on extra flexible necks so they can turn them in almost a complete circle. An owl can look right back over its own shoulders. Tests have shown that owls can find their food in total darkness.

Owls nest in the middle layers and on the ground, as well as in the canopy. They hunt in the evening and at night for almost the exact same food that hawks hunt for during the day—rats and mice, squirrels, snakes, frogs, insects, rabbits, moles, and so on.

Cottontail rabbit

Are hawks and owls cruel?

Some people think hawks and owls are cruel, but they are not. They live doing the job for which they are adapted. They hunt for small animals that reproduce in great numbers. In years when there are lots of rodents, more young hawks and owls live to grow up. In years when there are fewer, not so many hawks and owls develop into adults.

We may imagine that these birds are cruel, if we pretend to be the little rabbit that is being snatched up into the air, about to become food. Certainly we would hate to be the small mouse that gets swallowed by an owl. But while the death of these little animals may seem sad, try to imagine what the world would be like if there were no hawks or owls or other predators.

Mice, for example, have lots of babies every couple of weeks. If nothing at all happened to any of these babies, within a year there would be millions upon millions of mice scurrying around. Now mice don't live without eating, so the millions of mice would eat all the seeds from all the trees, all the grain from the fields, all the tender twigs and sprouts, and so on. Young trees would die because mice would eat off the bark. With so many hungry mice no plants would be left standing. It would be a total disaster.

Hawks and owls hunt for hours each day, but they don't manage to capture every mouse or rabbit or mole. Many of the healthiest ones escape. The animals that predators catch are often the weakest, slowest members of the group.

Owls and hawks don't hunt because they are cruel, but because that is what they must do in order to stay alive and reproduce their species. In doing so, they serve to keep the balance of nature. And while we may not like their work, we can still be grateful that they do it.

Screech owls

3 The Middle Layers

What are the middle layers?

It is the section of the forest that lies between the arch of canopy overhead and the ground cover at your feet. What you see there depends on what stage the forest has reached in its development. If it is a mature forest and no lumbermen have taken out the big trees, you may find the middle layers quite open. You will be able to walk with ease among the trees, for few shrubs or bushes grow in the dim light. If the forest has been lumbered over fairly recently and many of the big trees removed, the middle layers will be a dense jungle of plants competing to get into the open spaces where those trees once stood. There will be tangles of raspberry and blackberry bushes and other shrubs; vines; young trees and other rapidly growing plants. And if the forest is young with few tall trees in it, you are also likely to find it crowded and difficult to work your way through.

Rhododendron shrubs at the foot of tree trunks, along a stream bank in the Great Smoky Mountains in Tennessee

Dogwood tree

The middle layers of the forest has two stories, or levels. Immediately beneath the canopy is the understory. Here you will find the tops of trees that will, if they get the chance, eventually crowd up into the canopy, as well as those of smaller trees that will never grow that high. The lower story of the middle layers is the shrub layer, where thickets of bushes provide safe hideouts and good supplies of food for many forest animals.

In the middle layers, too, are the trunks of all the trees—giant pipelines from the soil to the leaves in the canopy. The bark on the trunks of trees provides a feeding ground for a number of birds, and the trunks of dead trees can be hollowed out for nesting places. The middle layers is far more than just an empty space between the canopy and the ground.

Not everyone who talks about this part of the forest speaks of the understory and the shrub layer. A person who is interested in birds thinks of the middle layers in terms of nesting places, perches, and territories, of low bushes, high bushes, small sap-

Dogwood

lings, lower branches of trees, and hollow trunks—each place being important to bird life.

What are some of the smaller trees found in the middle layers?

Gray and white birches, aspen, scrub oak, ironwood, hop hornbeam, black cherry, sassafras, alder, redbud, and dogwood are some of the smaller trees found in the middle layers of various woods. They grow in patches of sunlight, sometimes where trees have been cut down, and on the edge of the deep forest. Some of them, like dogwood, have snaky-looking branches that can grow sideways for quite a distance and thus obtain more light.

The white blossoms I found in the woods are from a dogwood tree. Are the similar pink blossoms I saw from a dogwood, too?

Yes, they are, and they are not flowers as many people think but modified leaves. The actual flowers of the dogwood are very small and not at all colorful. The true dogwood flowers grow in the middle of the showy bracts, as the modified leaves are called. Although the true dogwood flowers are themselves plain, after they have been fertilized, they develop into bright red berries. Dogwood berries feed many woodland creatures, including birds, deer, and mice.

Black cherry

I saw a tree with long white flower clusters and dark shiny leaves. What kind of tree was it?

It was probably a black cherry tree. In the spring the black cherry has soft white spikes of flowers. These later turn into berries, which first are red and then a shiny black. The bark of an old tree is black and scaly. The rough edges of the flat scales turn out a little away from the tree. A young tree has a gray or reddish-brown shiny bark, marked with horizontal slits called lenticels. These lenticels let gases move in and out of the bark. All black cherry trees have openings in their bark, of one shape or another, to allow air to pass in and out. Sometimes you will see the nests of tent caterpillars in a black cherry and be angered to watch the worms busily chewing away every leaf.

Birch trees

Why are so many white birch trees bent over?

Young white birches start off growing up very straight, but for some reason their main stems or trunks are more flexible than those of other trees. In winter when the branches become coated with heavy layers of ice, you will sometimes see birches bent over in beautiful arches that touch the ground. Cracks often open up in the bent-over trunks, and many birches never straighten up again after such a storm. When white birches remain bent over, the branches on their upper sides begin to grow straight up and look like the rows of trees crossing a bridge in a Japanese garden. Sometimes fungi get into a birch through these cracks. When that happens, a birch doesn't have very long to live.

How does a shrub differ from a tree?

A shrub, or bush, has a cluster of short woody stems springing up from the earth as a group. Each stem has short branches and carries its leaves a few feet above the ground. A set of roots gathers water and minerals for all the stems. A tree is also a woody plant, but it usually has only one important stem—the trunk.

Have there always been shrubs?

As did some of the smaller trees, many shrubs came into being during and after the great glacial periods. They filled up the empty spaces left by the retreating ice, marching out in front of the trees, into the wet boggy places left behind. The red osier and other small dogwood shrubs can be found in such boggy places today. One of them—the bunchberry—is a tiny woody

Bunchberry

shrub only a few inches high. It is found in northern coniferous and deciduous forests and in clear spaces around the edges and in open patches of spruce-fir woods.

I found a branch that had some pods with the seeds still inside. After I took it home and put it in my room, the pods began to explode in every direction. Why?

They must have been the seedpods of the shrub called witch hazel. They are so made that when the walls of the pods dry out and begin to change shape, a great deal of tension builds up. This tension becomes so great that finally the seedpods burst open along particular lines, and in your case the little nutlets were hurled across the room. The same thing happens in the forest, where the nutlets are thrown off from the adult plant. In this way the witch-hazel bush gets started in new places.

Other plant seeds are scattered in various ways. Some catch in animal fur and are carried a long way through the forest before they drop off. Others are borne by the wind on umbrellas of down or on tiny wings. Still others are eaten by birds or other animals to be deposited somewhere in the forest floor in a pile of animal dung.

I found some little pointed nuts hanging on a bush. What could they be?

You may have been lucky enough to have found some hazelnuts before the squirrels got to them. The hazelnut bush has been making nuts for some ten million years, before there were any squirrels around to eat them. Now the squirrels find them before the nuts are even ripe, so we rarely get the chance to eat any ourselves.

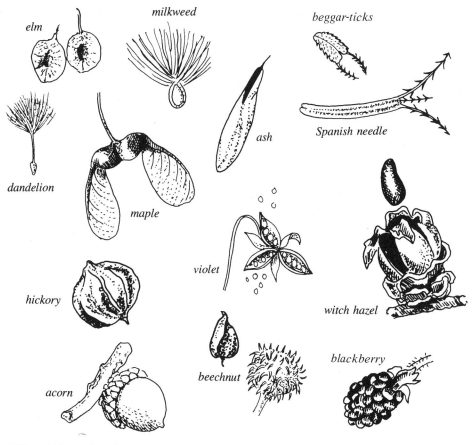

elm

milkweed

beggar-ticks

dandelion

maple

ash

Spanish needle

hickory

violet

witch hazel

acorn

beechnut

blackberry

Different kinds of seeds

The hazelnut is a shrub with many relatives, among them the birch trees, the American hornbeams, the hop hornbeams, and the alders. Alders are shrubs that grow in wet places, such as along the edges of streams and in swamps and bogs.

What is the bush whose flowers are like a yellow mist in spring?

The spicebush has yellow flowers like a fine mist in spring. And if you brush against the shrub and bruise its twigs, you will smell a nice spicy smell. If you chew on a twig or crush one of the plant's red berries, you will find that they have a spicy taste and smell. The spicebush belongs to the same family as the laurel.

I saw birds eating red berries off a bush in winter. What kind of bush holds its berries that long?

You have probably found a winterberry bush, a very important bush for birds that stay around in cold weather. Winterberry bushes are either male or female, so both kinds have to grow near each other in the forest for berries to develop on the female bush.

What is the name of the small shrub that has leaves like maple leaves and dark blue berries?

You must have found a maple-leaved viburnum. It has several very close relatives in the woods: the nannyberry or sheepberry—a much larger type—and the blackhaw. All of them have small white flowers that grow in flat clusters, and they all have dark blue fruits. Look for leaves and branches that grow opposite each other.

The wood of the viburnum is tough and flexible and was used for many things by the Indians: arrows, whips, hobbles, and strong baskets. The berries of some of these shrubs used to be dried and eaten like raisins.

What are those arching branches that grow close to the ground, the ones that trip you when you are in a hurry in the woods?

They are the branches of the hobblebush, which is also a

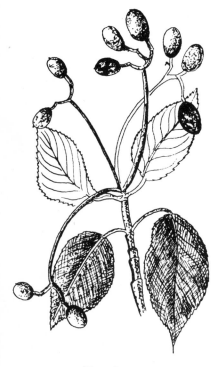

Nannyberry

The maple-leaved viburnum, which grows in abundance in deciduous forests in the eastern United States

viburnum. When they bend down and touch the ground, they take root. Then the newly rooted parts of the branch thicken and become new stems. The parts that are still connected to the original bush become a hobble, ready to trip you up if you don't happen to notice them. By rooting this way, the bush spreads across the ground.

If you don't happen to get tripped by the hobbles, you can still learn to tell the hobblebush by looking for its heart-shaped leaves. They have deep teeth and their undersides are coated with brownish hair. A hobblebush makes red fruits that later turn purple.

Hobblebush

Wintergreen

What made the leaves of a plant I found smell delicious, like wintergreen chewing gum?

The leaves of the wintergreen plant (*Gaultheria procumbens*) have an oil inside them that gives off a lovely smell when you crush the leaf. The leaves are shiny and tough, and grow on little stems about three or four inches high. Wintergreen is one of the smallest of the woody shrubs. Sometimes hanging below the leaf are a few little red berries that smell like teaberry gum when you crush them. The berry is edible.

The staghorn sumac, in fruit

I saw a fruit that looked like a little red cup with a black seed in it. What kind of berry was it?

It was probably the berry of the American yew, an evergreen shrub. When you go back to the woods, check the undersides of the twigs and needles to see if they are all the same color green. If it is a yew, the needles will also spiral around the twigs. The American yew has both male and female plants, so both must grow in the woods if berries are to form on the female shrub. The wood of the yew is good for making bows.

American yew

What was the name of the thick, red furry thing I found? It was heavy, too.

You perhaps found the fruited section of a shrub called the staghorn sumac. In winter the leaf scars along the stems of this plant almost surround the winter buds. In summer you find long leaves made up of many separate parts. Birds relish the fruit of the staghorn sumac, and people use it, too. A kind of lemonade can be made by soaking it in water, and then straining off the liquid.

What are those beautiful flowers that are shaped like tiny bowls and grow in clusters?

They are the fruit of the beautiful evergreen known as rhododendron. Rhododendrons are plants in the heath family, the same family as laurels, azaleas, blueberries, and huckleberries. The large flowers of the rhododendron are very beautiful, a kind of pinkish color, and the leaves are a dark waxy green. You will find the flowers in late June or July. The bush grows in terrifically dense thickets, the stems so close together that it is very hard to find a way through.

Rhododendron

The blossoms of the mountain laurel, a relative of the rhododendron. Its leaves are less than half as large as rhododendron leaves, and shinier.

I think I found some blueberries in the woods. Is that possible?

Yes, there are two main types of blueberry bushes in the woods, high bush blueberries and low bush blueberries. The flowers of the blueberry bloom in May and are either white or pink. Low bush blueberries are found along dry ledges in the woods. High bush blueberry bushes are four to ten feet high and have berries that are bigger and more delicious than those of the low bush type. Birds as well as bears and people like blueberries. In the fall the leaves of the blueberry bushes turn bright red or bronze.

Blueberry

I thought I found a blueberry, but it didn't taste very good. What was it?

Probably it was a huckleberry. They are very seedy and not as good as blueberries, although from the outside they look very much the same. If the leaves on the bush have yellow, sticky dots on their upper sides, it's a huckleberry.

Are there many bushes in the woods with fruits on them?

Yes. Besides the ones that have already been mentioned there are a number of others. Some have fruit that birds like; some have fruit that people hunt for. The shadbush, the raspberry, and the blackberry are several bushes that help feed woodland animals.

Are there any bushes with enough fruit on them to pick and make jam?

Yes, there are. Besides blueberry, raspberry, and blackberry bushes, you might try to find some elderberry bushes. They grow about ten to twelve feet tall. Some have green branches with white pith inside. There are lots of berries in each cluster, and they are purplish black. Another kind of elderberry has red berries and stems with brown pith inside.

TREE TRUNKS

When I was in the forest, there were tree trunks all around me. Why was the bark on many of them so rough?

The bark on the trunks of young trees and young branches

Blackberry

Elderberry

Trunks of the stately redwood tree growing along the coast of California, near Mill Creek. The redwoods are among our tallest and oldest conifers.

and twigs is rather smooth, but as the trees grow bigger and thicker, the bark splits apart, and cracks form. The cracks deepen as the trunks and branches grow stouter and push the sections of bark outward. Each different kind of tree has its own particular pattern of roughness. You can learn to recognize bark the way you learn to recognize faces—by small details. Even the smooth bark of the white birch begins to form patches of rough, blackish bark when it grows old. Like the young birch, the young sycamore tree has bark that is fairly smooth, too. But it throws off great pieces of bark as soon as its branches grow thicker than a quarter of an inch.

Can you take the bark off a tree? What is under it?

You can take the bark off, but you shouldn't. Many a tree has been killed because someone cut a ring around the trunk, digging through the bark into the living layers. This is called girdling the tree, and pioneers used to do it as the first step in clearing land for farming. Once the bark has been cut and the cambium and sapwood exposed, the tree begins to die.

The cambium and sapwood are the living layers of the tree. It is the cambium that adds new wood cells to the girth of the tree, layer after layer. Each year it makes new cells toward the inside and the outside.

On the inner side of the cambium is the sapwood. It is made up mostly of cells called xylem cells, which conduct water up from the roots to the leaves. Beyond the sapwood, in the center of the trunk, is a deeper layer called the heartwood. It helps to make the trunk more rigid and contains deposits of tree gums and resins.

Cross section of a young tree trunk

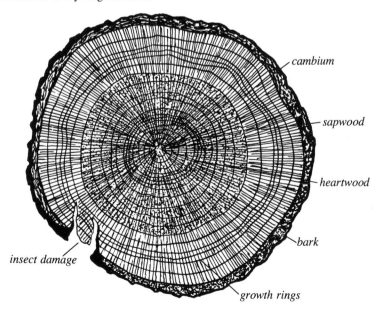

cambium

sapwood

heartwood

bark

insect damage

growth rings

On the outside of the cambium is a layer of cells called phloem cells. They conduct the food-containing sap up and down the tree. Beyond the phloem cells are dead cork cells. These and some of the old phloem cells make up the bark.

Bark is waterpoof because of a substance in the cork cells called suberin. Bark insulates the cambium against sudden changes in temperature and from the heat of sunlight and ground fires. Some rough bark lets quite a bit of air through it to the cells of the cambium. But being very waterpoof, it prevents too much water from the sapwood being lost to the air.

A photomicrograph of a young twig of the tulip tree. A twig is a branch with only a year or two of growth in it.

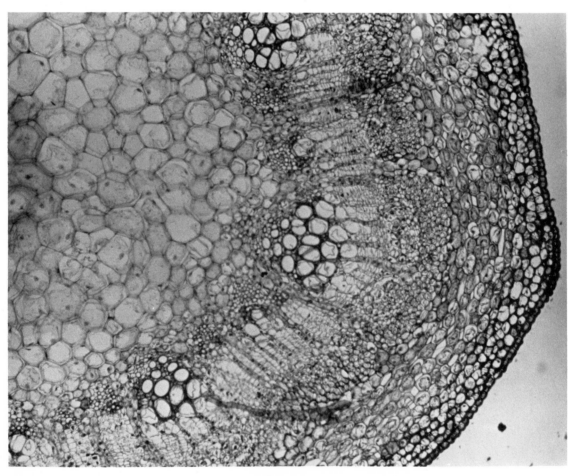

Why is a tree trunk round?

A tree trunk is round, although not always perfectly round, because the cambium cells in the trunk divide at about the same time and grow at about the same rate. A tree does not grow more on one side than another, unless something has influenced it, such as the wind or the pull of gravity, if it's a leaning tree, or the light shining more on one side than the other. Most trees that are forced to lean over for a long time will grow more on the underside, making that side stronger, and the trunk will not be round. A tree that has branches growing out equally on all sides is the most perfectly round.

Why do some trunks have a green side?

Whenever you see a greenish tinge on a tree trunk, you can be reasonably certain that there are green plants of some sort or another living on it, on the side of the tree that's dampest. Some of the plants that give a tree tunk a green look—green algae, for example—are too small to be seen clearly with the eyes alone. The help of a microscope is needed.

Larger plants also grow on tree trunks, though. Sometimes you will find smooth moss clinging to the bark or scaly gray-green lichens. Lichens are curious flat, mossy, or leafy things of a blue-green tint (or other pastel shade of yellow-green, orange, or tan) made up of two kinds of organisms living together: an alga and a fungus. You may not find lichens on a young tree, for they take several years to grow to a noticeable size.

What happens when lightning strikes a tree trunk?

Sometimes nothing happens, but occasionally . . . zap! millions of volts of electricity zip down the juicy cambium layer

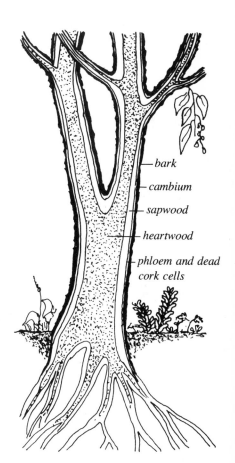

bark

cambium

sapwood

heartwood

phloem and dead cork cells

Vertical or long section of a tree

that is just under a tree's bark. The sap is heated to the boiling point, and a long strip of bark is ripped to pieces by a violent explosion of steam. From top to bottom a section of the tree is laid naked along a jagged lightning-shaped crack. Sometimes it is split into big hunks of wood. Don't stand under the tallest tree during an electric storm, for that is the tree the lightning is likely to strike.

I saw a small shelf sticking out from the trunk of a dead tree. What was it?

Small, medium, and large shelves often stick out from the trunks of dead trees. Some of them hug closely to the tree trunk, while others grow out from it on stalks. These ''shelves'' are polypore bracket fungi. Sometimes they look more like mushrooms than shelves. You can tell the two apart because the polypore bracket fungi have thousands of holes dotting their undersides. The word *polypore* means many holes.

Another kind of bracket fungus, the shellac fungus, grows mainly on the stumps of hemlock trees, where it finds certain substances it needs for life. It is stalked and has a shiny reddish-brown top and a straw-colored underside.

Do fungi grow on living trees, too?

Bracket fungi often grow on living trees that have been injured in some way. The spores of the fungi get into the tree through the wound and begin to grow, sinking their rootlike cables—called rhizomorphs—into the wood of the tree. The wood begins to rot, and the fungus is fed. Soon the fungus shows itself on the outside of the tree.

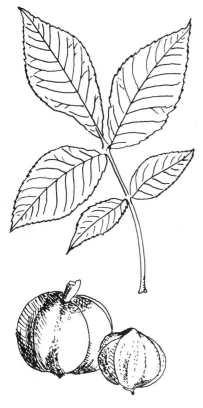

Shagbark hickory

A lot of young trees die because they are attacked by fungi. And when an old tree dies, it is usually for that reason.

I saw a tree with shaggy-looking bark. What kind of tree was it?

You have probably found a hickory tree, common in the eastern woodlands. Together with the oak, it sometimes makes up entire forests. The hickory tree has a nut with a neat four-part shell, and leaves that have seven to nine leaflets to the group. Hickory nuts, along with acorns, are an important source of food for many woodland animals.

Trunks of the shagbark-hickory tree (left) and the pitch pine

Why does the bark of a birch peel so easily?

Birch bark is something like tissue paper. There are separate layers of it, and each layer is very thin. As the tree grows, the bark splits open, but it does not split all the way around the trunk in special patterns like other bark. It splits mostly along one side, making it easy to grab and strip off. The layers of birch bark don't lock into each other the way the layers of most other barks do.

On a tree such as the birch it is only too easy to start pulling what seems like a dead strip and then suddenly find yourself all the way down to the juicy cambium. If you want to peel off a piece of birch bark, be absolutely sure it is a dead piece.

The bark of the black birch, which does not peel as easily as that of the white birch. On the right the bark has grown over and sealed a wound where a branch broke off.

LIFE ON ROCKS

Some of the plants growing on the faces of cliffs and other rocky outcroppings in the woods look different from plants that grow elsewhere in the forest. Are they different?

Yes, some are plants you will find only on rocks. Others are simply more noticeable when they are growing on the steep sides of rocks than when they are hidden among other plants on the forest floor. Plants that grow on rocks are plants that can afford to dry up sometimes and still survive, or that need very little soil or light. Thus you will see lichens and liverworts and particular kinds of mosses and ferns. On places on the rocks that are very smooth, only lichens and moss can take hold. Other places are streaked with dirt-filled cracks and grooves. The more dirt the rock has and the more sunlight it gets, the more plants you will find living there.

Why are some rocky places very green and others pink or orange? What does this color come from?

Every rock has its own color, which is the color of the minerals in it. As soon as a rock is exposed to the air for any length of time, its color may change. Oxygen often attacks the surface minerals, especially those containing iron, and makes them darker and redder or browner.

Plants give color to rocks, too. Some rocks look as if they had been painted shades of pink, orange, green, gray, and blue-green. The green color may be the color of algae or of a small crusty lichen. The pink or orange color is caused by another kind of crusty lichen. Or the rock may be covered with a thick carpet of dark-green or even blackish moss.

Crustose lichens growing on a granite boulder in the Pocono Mountains of Pennsylvania

Although they often look rather dead, algae, lichens, and moss are all living things. Scientists have tests to show this. Certain of the tests for life measure the oxygen that plant cells use to stay alive. Plants take in oxygen either through the thin cell wall on the outside of the plant or through the pores on the leaf, first, and then through the cell wall. One way you can tell something is alive is by the fact that it uses oxygen.

Living plants not only use oxygen, but they give it off when bright light shines on them. The oxygen given off by photosynthesis can be measured, too. Thus, scientists have two good ways to prove to themselves that algae, mosses, and lichens are alive, even when they do not look very lively.

Stuck up there on the rocks were things that had the size and shape of giant potato chips. What were they?

They are lichens called rock tripe (*Umbilicaria*). When they are dry, they are crisp and easily snapped. When they are wet, they are flabby but tough, and a little greener.

Lichens are plants created by a working partnership of two very different groups of plants—the algae and the fungi. The algae make food by photosynthesis, which the fungi absorb. The fungi contribute by secreting "lichen acids" that work on the rock, dissolving some minerals in it that are used by the algae.

In rock tripe and in most typical lichens, a species of blue-

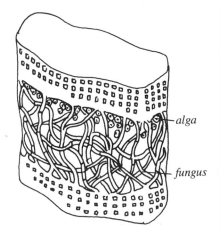

Algal and fungal cells in a lichen

Rock tripe, a foliose lichen, growing on a very shaded cliff in the Berkshire Hills of Massachusetts

green alga lives among the tangled threads of the fungus. Living together like this is a type of symbiosis where each organism benefits from the presence of the other.

Rock tripe has been used by starving people lost in the wilds to make soup. It makes a tasteless soup with very little nutritive value, but perhaps enough to save a life. Lichens are sensitive to air pollution and die after a year or two if exposed to sulfur dioxide.

Different kinds of lichens

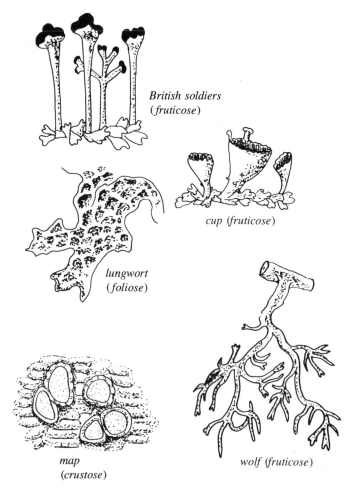

British soldiers
(*fruticose*)

cup (*fruticose*)

lungwort
(*foliose*)

map
(*crustose*)

wolf (*fruticose*)

What are those tiny green things on the rocks, the ones with red tips? They look like little matchsticks.

They are a fruticose lichen, sometimes called "British soldiers." The red tips are the spore-making part of the lichen, called podetia. Lichens occur in three general types: leathery and leafy (the foliose type), brittle and scaly (the crustose type), and bushy or stalked with little cups (the fruticose type).

I found some dried-up, blackish-looking dead moss on a rock. Did it die for lack of water?

Moss sometimes looks so dry you might well think it was dead, but it is not. If it rains, it will swell up, turn green again, and start to grow a little.

In the woods I discovered some water seeping down a cliff from a hidden spring. Many tiny green plants grew in the trickle. Are they special kinds?

Yes, and they look like moss plants, but they are not. If you got up very close to them or looked at them through a magnifying glass, you could see that the leaves are arranged differently from those on a moss plant; they overlap each other more. These plants are in a group of their own, called the leafy liverworts, recognized by their spore capsules and special leaf shape.

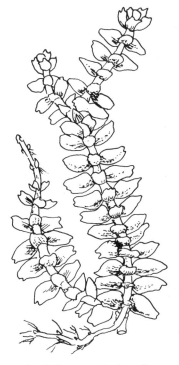

What are those scaly-looking things I sometimes see at the wet bases of cliffs?

These are liverworts, too, but of a flat rather than a leafy kind. There are many liverworts that are not leafy, and they are

Leafy liverwort (enlarged)

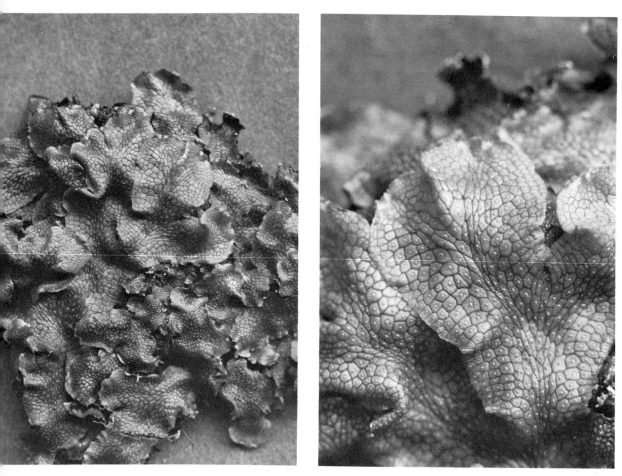

The thallose liverwort, *Conocephalum,* a very common inhabitant of wet places in the forest. The little polygonal areas—they show most clearly in the magnified view to the right—are not individual cells, but consist of many cells. The holes in the middle of each area are air pores.

called the thallose liverworts. Their flat pads are truly liverish in shape, though they're green in color, sometimes tinged with edges of purple. Some of the leafy liverworts can dry up and then come back to life again when they are damp. The flat or thallose liverworts, however, are used to living where it's wet, and if they dry out, they may die.

Some ferns seem to grow out of rocks. How do they live there?

Several kinds of fern grow on rocks in the woods, most of them where there is a crack or cranny in the walls. Ferns send their tough, slender black or dark-brown roots into the cracks and find moisture and mineral nutrients there. There is always a little soil in the cracks, which you can see if you look rather closely. It may have taken that much soil many years to get there. Some of it was washed down from up above, and some was blown there by the wind. Part of it was made by other plants that lived and died on the rock, and part was made by the action of frost, which split off tiny pieces of rock.

The spleenwort fern, *Asplenium bradleyi,* lives on cliffs. It has a dark brown midrib, or rachis, down the center of each leaf, and very delicate leaflets. A fern called the walking fern lives on the faces of rocky ledges of limestone. When the tips of the leaves of this fern touch the cliff they take root and form a new plant. Another fern that lives on rocks, *Cystopteris bulbifera,* has baby ferns growing along the edges of the fronds. These break off and make new plants.

A fern on a large rock or on the side of a cliff fastens itself there with threadlike roots, which are covered all over with root hairs. The roots make a mat, and tiny bits of leaves are caught by it. Dirt washes into the mat and is held there. In this way a thin covering of soil is held to the rocks, and new ferns and other small plants can eventually grow in it.

ANIMALS OF THE MIDDLE LAYERS

When I was in the forest, flies kept dipping in and out of the sunbeams and wheeling around my head. What kind were they?

The list of flies in the woods is long, for the order *Diptera,* to

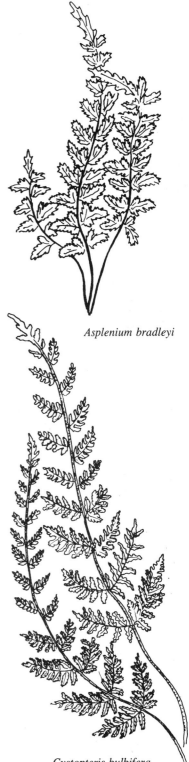

Asplenium bradleyi

Cystopteris bulbifera

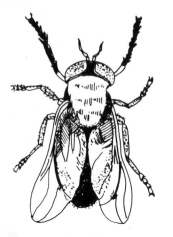

Horsefly

Female sawfly

Sawfly larva

which all true flies belong, is one of the largest groups of insects. Among those that you may see or hear in the middle layers, or in other parts of the woods for that matter, are dung flies, deerflies, flower flies, fruit flies, leaf-miner flies, minute black scavenger flies, horseflies, blackflies, midges, and mushroom flies—among others! Dragonflies, sawflies, caddis flies, and stone flies are not true flies. They have four wings, and true flies have only two. Behind the two wings of true flies is a pair of balancing organs. These are little stalks with knobs, called halteres.

Of all the flies listed above the most destructive is the sawfly. The female sawfly lays her eggs in plant leaves. To get them inside, she saws open the leaf with two blades that she has at her rear end. The larvae that hatch from the eggs destroy the leaf tissue. One type of sawfly has done lots of damage to spruce trees in northern forests. The only way known to control this pest is to import parasites from Europe that kill sawflies. Also it is hoped that birds that eat sawflies may be encouraged to live in these woods, although encouraging a bird is not an easy job! Sawflies attack all kinds of conifer and broadleaf trees, and they do a lot of damage.

How many leaves can a tent caterpillar eat?

Lots, but it would be hard to say exactly how many unless you put a caterpillar in a jar and counted the leaves you gave it. You can find the whitish tents of these creatures in small trees and shrubs in the middle layers of the forest. They may be as much as several feet long and a foot wide. The caterpillars stay in their weblike nest for the night and travel out along the branches to feed during the day. They start as tiny creatures and grow and grow and grow, before they spin cocoons and transform themselves into moths. A large tent of caterpillars can clean the leaves right off a tree.

Who eats tent caterpillars?

A number of birds eat them, one of which is the yellow-billed cuckoo. If you are very lucky, you might see this brownish-backed bird standing on a limb, pecking away at a nest of tent caterpillars. The yellow-billed cuckoo is a little larger than a robin. It has a white breast and an extra-long tail with black-and white tipped feathers. Its bill is black above and yellow below. Its feet are a little different from those of most birds—with two toes pointing ahead and two behind. (Most birds have three toes pointing ahead and one pointing behind.)

When I peeled the bark off a dead pine tree, I found tunnels in the wood underneath it. How were they made?

The tunnels were probably made by pine-bark beetles, which killed the tree by eating too much of the living cambium and young sapwood. A male beetle tunnels into the pine tree first and makes a hollow. Females follow him, each making a tunnel for itself in which to lay eggs. The little larvae that hatch from the eggs eat out their own tunnels and grow. The wood they eat is food for them. When they become adults, they gnaw their way out through the bark and fly off to find new trees. These beetles damage and kill lots of pine trees. Most kinds of trees are attacked by one variety of bark beetle or another but usually not enough beetles attack trees to kill them.

What does a woodpecker find in the bark it pecks?

Bark beetles are not the only things that move under the bark

Tent caterpillars

Yellow-billed cuckoo

Holes made in an ash tree by a pileated woodpecker

of a tree, and a woodpecker knows it. There are larvae of other insects lurking in tunnels and gnawing their way through the wood of the tree. The woodpecker props itself against the tree, clinging to it with its claws and leaning on its tail which has spiky feathers. Like most birds, the woodpecker has four toes on each foot. Unlike most birds but like those of the yellow-billed cuckoo, its feet have two toes pointing forward and two back, so the woodpecker can get a good grip on the bark. Turning its head this way and that, it seems to hear the larvae eating. When the woodpecker knows where a larva is, it drills a hole through the bark and finds the tunnel where it is. Then it stretches out its long tongue and spears the grub right there in its hole.

Woodpeckers drill out large holes in decaying trees and make nests in them. They don't live in young forests, for they need old and dying trees for both food and nesting places. There is more food under the bark of old trees.

When a woodpecker is signaling, rather than eating, it raps on the tree with a much louder sound.

Red-headed woodpecker

Do any other birds live in the holes and hollows of old trees?

Yes, not only woodpeckers make nest in holes and hollows. The great crested flycatcher and the screech owl, among others, nest in old woodpecker holes or other hollows. Chickadees dig out holes in stumps, trunks, and branches. When the woods have been cleared of old trees, there are fewer places for these birds.

I saw some little birds using a tree trunk as a circular staircase. Were they playing?

No. They were probably looking for food in the bark—ants, spiders, sawflies, and other insects that might be hiding in some of the cracks. A bird called a brown creeper goes up the trunks of trees in a regular spiral, hopping, propping itself up with its

Brown creeper

Chickadee

Gray catbird

tail, and searching out food with its long bill. The pine warbler creeps up and down, all over pine trees, growing dirty with pine pitch as it looks for food.

I saw a group of little gray birds with black caps and white bibs fly into a bush. What were they?

They were almost surely chickadees. If it was winter, you might well have seen some other kinds of birds traveling along with them in their search for food. Woodpeckers, nuthatches, and creepers band together with chickadees in the winter. Chickadees eat a diet of about 70 percent insects and 30 percent vegetable matter. It's hard to imagine how many insects chickadees eat in a single day. A scientist estimated, after careful observation, that one chickadee ate over one hundred thousand cankerworm eggs in about twenty-five days. And that's probably not all the bird ate. It takes a lot of flying, hopping, pecking, nibbling, and swallowing to eat such a huge number of eggs. It's not surprising that birds use up most of the energy they get from their food.

When I was in the forest, I thought I heard a kitten mewing, but I couldn't find it. What was it?

When catbirds call, they sound like mewing cats. They also sing, and their song is very lovely. Catbirds live near the ground, in the low trees and shrubs of the middle layers, in nests strung with grapevines. Catbirds eat all kinds of berries, including poison-ivy berries, and they also eat beetles, grasshoppers, and crickets.

Birds and other animals that eat berries usually don't digest the hard seeds that lie inside the fruit. These seeds are passed out with other wastes, and coated with a little bit of fertilizer, they have a good chance of growing in the new spot.

I poked my hand into a crack in a rock and got my fingers covered with a sticky cobweb. Do spiders live among rocks?

You find spiders living in the cracks of rocks and on the plants that sometimes grow out of them, as well as in houses, in fields, and among trees and other plants throughout the forest.

All spiders can spin silk, but not all of them use this talent to the same extent. It all depends on the life they lead. For some spiders, the thread they spin is as important to their life as a rope is to a rock climber on a mountainside, for it helps them to travel conveniently across the airy space where they hunt their prey. Many spiders by spinning webs use their silk to capture food. Others do not make webs.

Spiders are able to spin silk before they even emerge from the egg sac. And as soon as they hatch, they start to attach lines at various points to whatever they are upon. The piece of silk you see on a branch or twig could be one of many kinds, for spiders spin different types of silk. They spin one kind for ballooning, for long trips through the air at the end of a silken line. They spin another type for webs, and yet another to package their prey. Some of these threads are too fine for our eyes to see. For catching prey, not all spiders make the familiar circular web with silken spirals. Some spiders just cast out a small snarl or fashion a funnel of silk. And others stalk their prey without any silk at all.

Are any spiders dangerous?

Yes. Before you thrust your hand into a crack in a rock to

A silk spider

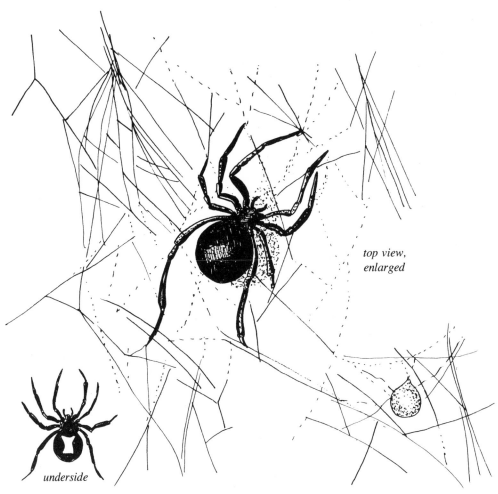

top view, enlarged

underside

Black widow spider

feel what's inside, take a good look first. Shine a flashlight inside if necessary. You wouldn't want to disturb a black widow or a violin spider in their hideouts. The black widow is the more common of the two kinds of dangerous spiders. It is found in both the eastern and western United States. The violin spider is the more rare of the two. Other spiders besides these will sometimes ''bite,'' but most are not strong enough to puncture the human skin with their two fangs.

How do spiders use the prey they catch?

They use it not by biting it and chewing it but by sucking the juice out of it. They have mouth parts that suck, rather than bite and chew. Spiders are an important part of the food chain because they prey on insects, whether by stalking them and leaping upon them as do the wolf spiders or by merely trapping them as do the orb-weaver spiders. If you come across a spider's web in the woods, watch to see what happens in it but don't destroy it.

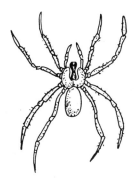

Violin spider

4 The Ground Cover

What is the ground cover?

If you've been in the forest long enough to discover a place where violets grow or to trip on a bed of moss, then you have already begun to notice the ground cover. Up and over the hill, skirting around the bases of rocks and winding in between tree trunks, grow a great variety of small plants. Those that appear early in the spring are very noticeable because so few other plants as yet have leaves. There are two very different types of plants in the ground cover. Some have flowers that bear seeds; others do not have flowers that bear seeds but give rise to a dusty spore cloud. The ferns, the club mosses, the true mosses, and the horsetails, for example, start new plants from tiny spores instead of seeds.

The leaves of the Canada Mayflower, a small perennial plant that blooms in early spring. It belongs to the lily family.

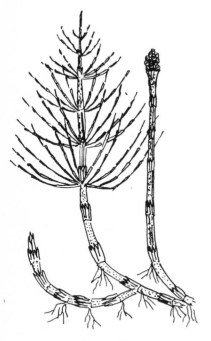

Horsetails

In certain places in the forest the plants of the ground cover will tear at your ankles with nettles or thorns; in other places they will brush your legs like soft feathers. Perhaps you will find a bed of club moss spread over the ground, tempting you to feel its furry tips and pick the little cones that poke up above them. Perhaps you will fan yourself with a fern frond plucked from a large crown. As you look, you will notice first a few, then more and still more kinds of plants growing close around you. And if you are lucky, you may spot one of the animals that hunts and hides on the ground.

Why are there lots of green plants in some places and none in others?

This depends on several things, but most of all on how much light filters down to the ground and on the kind of soil present in a particular spot. Each kind of plant has taken millions of years to develop in the way it has—through the process of evolution. Each has its own peculiar chemistry and its own particular way of life. Each type of plant needs a certain soil, light intensity, and amount of humidity.

For example, most plants that grow under broadleaf trees don't do well under pines or spruces, for the soil under conifers is different and the shade all the year around is greater. The flowering plants of early spring would not get the light they need under a stand of pines.

If you find a place in the woods where there are not many plants, you can probably figure out the reason. First check to see how much light reaches that spot and the kinds of leaves on the trees. Then, feel the soil to see if it is dry. Aside from requiring just the right soil, light intensity, and humidity, woodland plants need plenty of water.

FLOWERING PLANTS OF THE GROUND COVER

Why do the flowering plants of the ground cover become green before the trees?

As the sun's angle steepens in the spring, the hours of daylight grow longer and the air becomes warmer. Soon the snow melts and the top layer of earth warms up a bit. The earth warms, first of all, on the hillsides facing south.

Under the soil in the forest lie seeds, roots, and rhizomes—rootlike plant stems—that are sensitive to the new warmth and the longer days. When the light and temperature are right for them, they awaken. Before the leaves have begun to show on the big trees above them, the small, soft-stemmed plants begin to grow, spread their leaves, make flowers and then seeds, and start to store food.

Gradually sap surges up into the branches to awaken the buds of the trees. These buds open, and they soon make such an umbrella of leaves overhead that most of the light is shut off from the forest floor. The small plants settle down to a quiet spell. They don't grow much anymore, but some do continue slowly to make and store food in the roots and rhizomes underground. They will use the stored food for growing and flowering the following spring.

The small flowering plants can use the sunlight and the warmth very early in the spring, in that brief period of time before the trees fill out with leaves. This is called adaptation—they have developed a special way of life that helps them survive.

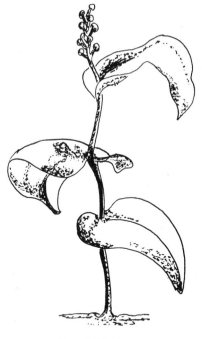

Canada Mayflower

How long do these flowering plants live?

The soft-stemmed flowering plants have different life spans.

Some of them grow in a single summer, make flowers and seeds, and then die. These are called annuals. Others, which take two summers to produce seeds, have some kind of a food-storage organ to tide them over the first winter. They die at the end of the second summer. These are called biennials. And still another group sends up its shoots during the summer and produces seeds every year. In the fall this kind of plant dies back to its storage organ, which may be either thick fleshy roots or a horizontal rhizome that lies flat against the ground or just underground. The roots and rhizomes send up new leaves and flowers when the weather gets warm again the next year. Plants that produce seeds year after year are called perennials.

Why do plants have flowers?

Flowers are the reproductive organs of plants. Their function is to make seeds from which new plants will grow.

What are the little spikes and clubs in the middle of a flower?

The tiny spikes and clubs that poke up inside the circle of petals are the reproductive organs of the plant. They are the parts that together help make the seeds that will become new plants.

If you look closely you will find two different kinds of spikes—male and female. In some flowers they are not too hard to tell apart. The male parts are called stamens. They are usually long and thin from top to bottom, and swell at the tip into a little double sac called an anther. Once in a while the anther is on a short spike and looks more like a club, but you can still see the two parts of the pollen sac. Pollen grains by the hundreds—and sometimes thousands—are made inside of each

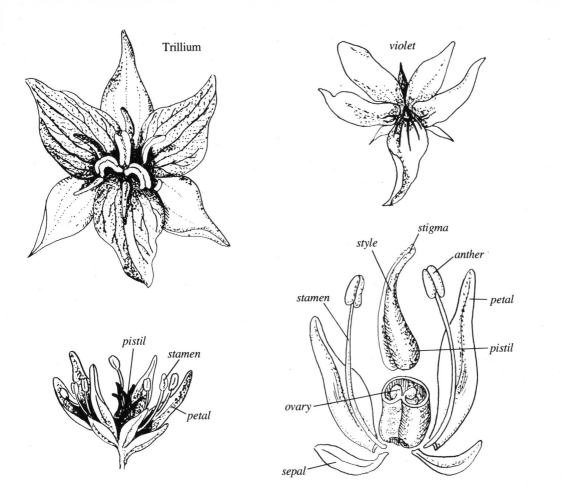

Trillium

violet

stigma

style

anther

stamen

petal

pistil

ovary

sepal

pistil

stamen

petal

Two typical flowers and two views of the parts of a flower

sac. These grains hold the sperm cells that will later pollinate the eggs in female flowers. Through fertilization—the bringing together of the sperm cells and the eggs—seeds that will eventually start new plants are formed.

The female spikes are called pistils. The pistil is a thicker spike than a stamen, especially down at the base where you find the ovary with the ovules inside. The ovule or young seed is where the plant makes eggs. These are not huge like chicken eggs. They are merely tiny cells that become embryos if they are fertilized. The spike sticking up above the ovary is called the style. At its tip is a sticky-looking landing place designed to catch flying pollen grains. This sticky place is called the stigma. When a pollen grain lands on the stigma, it is caught there, and if it is the right kind of pollen, it sends out a long slender tube. The pollen tube, with the sperm nucleus inside it, makes its way down through the style to an ovule in the ovary and fertilizes the egg. That starts the seed growing.

Do all flowers have a smell?

No, they don't. The flowers of oak and willows and quite a few other trees do not, and they depend on the wind to send their pollen grains to other flowers. Many flowers, however, do have a scent that attracts insects and even birds to them. These creatures visit flowers to get the nectar that is hidden among the petals. Nectar is a sugary liquid. If you have ever tried sipping

Skunk cabbage, one of the earliest plants to bloom in the spring. Only the witch hazel can claim an earlier blooming date.

from a honeysuckle flower, you know how good nectar tastes.

As the insects and birds drink, they pick up bits of pollen on their bodies. When they visit other flowers, they leave behind some of it, and in this way, they help to pollinate flowers without knowing they are doing a service.

Some flowers attract insects not by smell but by their showy colors, and some by the patterns formed by their petals. A few flowers depend on birds and even bats for pollination, but far more—about half the plants in the world that have pollen in them—depend on insects.

Skunk cabbage

In the woods, in swampy places, a maroon-colored flowering plant pokes up from the ground very early in the spring. If you disturb it or break it open, it smells like a skunk. What is it?

The plant is called a skunk cabbage. It grows in the deep mud of swampy land with long slender roots that go down a yard or more. Under the mud it has a thick rhizome that keeps it alive over the winter. In the spring, in some places as early as January, the hooded flower mass pops up, followed by the large, cabbagelike green leaves. The flower mass looks like the flower mass of the Jack-in-the-pulpit, only it is somewhat larger. So much heat is generated by the hood as it pushes up through the snow that it can actually hasten the melting of the snow around it. Skunk cabbage was used in days gone by as a potherb, which means that it was boiled in a pot and eaten like a vegetable, or used as a food seasoning.

How did the Jack-in-the-pulpit get its name?

It is called Jack-in-the-pulpit because of the way the hooded

Jack-in-the-pulpit, a relative of the familiar house plant philodendron

flower mass looks. Standing up firmly under an arched green canopy is the little club-shaped flower mass. Half of it is hidden by the folded hood around it, but enough of it shows to make it seem as if a very small preacher is giving his Sunday morning sermon from the pulpit. The "Jack" who is preaching is actually a stem covered with small flowers. The green and maroon pulpit is actually a highly modified leaf of the plant. The bunches of bright red, fruit-covered seeds of the plant are eaten by hungry pheasants and thrushes.

Energy for the new spring growth of the Jack-in-the-pulpit has been stored over the winter in an underground corm—a swollen stem that unlike a rhizome is quite fat and solid. This is one of the early plants up in the spring, and like the skunk cabbage, it thrives in wet places.

I saw a flower that looked like a violet, but it was yellow. What sort of flower was it?

It was undoubtedly a violet, albeit a yellow one. You can often find a number of yellow violets in the woods, as well as some white and some purple ones. The cultivated violet, or pansy, comes in many colors, too. Violets arise in the spring from rhizomes. These underground horizontal stems contain stored food, and as in many other plants, the leaves and flowers have been ready to grow, held in the bud, since the previous fall.

Each violet has nectar in it, but bees come to the flower partly because of its color. Bees bring pollen to each blossom, and soon seeds are growing inside the flower. Some violet plants don't make seeds in the bright flower only. If you look carefully down under the leaves of certain plants, you will find small green pods on slender stalks. Inside are flower buds without petals. In fact these flowers never open, and bees do not visit them, but within the pods seeds form anyhow, for the flower buds pollinate themselves. This do-it-yourself method is called cleistogamy.

Common purple violet

Rue anemone

Trillium

What other flowers can I find in the forest in early spring?

Anemones, or windflowers, with their white flowers are commonly found in the woods then. The rue anemone is sometimes up as early as March. It grows about nine inches high. Its flowers blossom in groups of three, each one opening separately. Anemones depend on insects that are out early in the spring to bring pollen to them.

What are the pretty, three-pointed single flowers that are borne on stalks with three leaves?

Those flowers, also up early in the spring, are members of the group called *Trillium*. Each plant has only one flower, white with a pink center in one variety or just plain white in another. One species, stinking Benjamin (*Trillium erectum*), smells like rotting meat. All trilliums grow from rhizomes, underground stems.

What was the plant I saw that had a long stalk and long skinny leaves?

It could have been some kind of grass, or it could have been a sedge or rush. It is very hard to tell these three kinds of plants apart. Despite the fact that grasses grow all over the world, and are one of the most important groups of plants for people—giving us corn, wheat, rye, barley, oats, and rice—grasses are really not very common in the woods. They don't grow well in shade.

To identify a grass plant, look for a round, hollow, jointed stem. The base of the leaves wraps around it in a sheath. The grass flower is one of the simplest of flowers, having no petals or sepals, just a pistil in female and stamens in male flowers.

Although the seeds on grasses in the woods are small, they are eaten by birds and small animals. Grass plants have underground stems that help to bind the soil together where they grow.

If the plant you found had grasslike leaves with several main veins, and it also had a triangular stem, you may have found the sedge (*Carex platyphylla*). This is a plant that flowers early in the springtime.

Another plant with a grasslike look is the rush (*Luzula campestris*). It has leaves like a grass plant, but its flowers are like miniature lilies. The seeds, or nutlets, that are formed by the rush are each just a little bigger than a pinhead, and each one has a tiny knob. Ants run up the flower stalk, grab these sweet little nutlets by the knobs, and carry them off to eat. Some of the nutlets stored in the ants' nest will not be eaten, however, and may turn into new rush plants.

(Left to right) Sedge, grass, and rush

Wild ginger, one of the first plants to bloom on sunny hillsides in the spring

I found a plant that smelled like a gingersnap. What was it?

It is called wild ginger (*Asarum canadense*), and some people make a candy with its root. They say it tastes delicious.

I found a plant that smelled like an onion. What was it?

It was an onion, a wild one. Some wild onions taste very good, and others don't because they are so strong. But there is no harm in trying the taste of any onion you find in the woods. The wild leek (*Allium tricoccum*) is good in soup.

I broke a leaf off a plant, and red juice came out of the stem. It looked like blood. What was it?

Certain plants have a colored, cloudy liquid in them, and the bloodroot plant, which is undoubtedly what you picked, is one of them. Under the ground the bloodroot has a rhizome that is full of this red juice. The juice is also found in the leaf stalk and flower stalk, above ground.

Like the trunks and branches of trees, the stems and branches of most land plants larger than the mosses have a xylem system, which carries water from root to shoot, and a phloem system, which carries food. Some plants, such as the bloodroot, have a third conducting or carrying system that contains a different kind of liquid, called latex. Latex is a rather thick, milky juice which most likely heals wounds when the plant is damaged.

Milkweed stems and pods and the Brazilian rubber tree have a lot of this liquid. A common plant called the celandine, a member of the poppy family, also has the juice, as do members of the lettuce family, some of which are found growing around the fringes of the forest or in clearings.

Bloodroot, *Sanguinaria canadensis,* another early spring plant

What makes some leaves furry?

Leave that feel furry are covered with tiny hairs. These hairs don't grow the way human hairs do, as pure protein strands made in clusters of cells called hair follicles. Plant hairs are made of cells that grow out of the surface of the leaf. Sometimes a plant hair is made of a single cell, sometimes of a whole chain of cells. The hair on our heads is dead, but plant hair is alive.

No one knows for sure why some leaves are hairy, but people have made some very good guesses. The hairs may protect the leaves from heating by scattering the light that lands on them. Or the hairs may keep the leaves from drying out too fast as the wind sweeps by. Possibly insects don't like eating the hairs, and so they stay away from the plant. And, surely, nettle plants with their stinging hairs keep enemies away (although there are people who eat young nettle leaves, after removing the hairs by boiling).

How do nettle plants sting?

The hairs on the leaves and stems of the stinging nettle plant have brittle glasslike tips that break off easily when you brush against them. After the needle tip is broken, a very sharp point is left on the hair. At the base of each hair is a bulb containing a liquid that is strongly irritating to human skin. When you bump against the nettle plant, some of the liquid is forced out of the plant hair into your skin. And how it burns! Of course, the stinging hairs of the nettle affect other animals in the same way. There are large patches of nettles in the woods, so watch out for them.

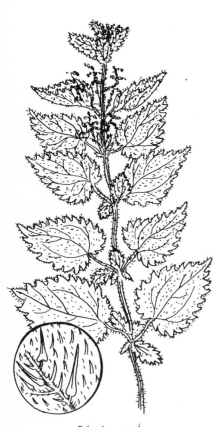

Stinging nettle

Poison sumac

Why do the leaves of poison ivy give me a rash?

The leaves of the poison-ivy plant and the stems and roots, too, have a chemical in them that raises blisters on the human skin. Not absolutely everyone gets these blisters, and some people get them worse than others. The chemical can float through the air when the plant is disturbed, so that some people cannot even pass a patch of poison ivy without getting a rash. When poison ivy is burned, a lot of the poison floats up, so beware! Danger!

Poison sumac can also give you a very uncomfortable rash.

CLUB MOSSES, FERNS, AND TRUE MOSSES

When I picked a plant that looked like a tiny fir tree, I got a whole string of little "trees." Why?

All the little "trees" are part of one plant that spreads across the forest floor by a rhizome that lies just under the surface of the ground. There are many plants that grow in this way, but the club mosses, which are not true mosses at all, are the ones that look a lot like miniature fir trees. The botanist who first named them thought that some species looked like little wolf's feet at the branch tips. Wolf's foot is what the generic scientific name, *Lycopodium,* means. As the rhizome grows horizontally along the surface of the ground, roots push down, and small green branches grow up all along it.

Lycopodium plants have been on earth for over 350 million years. They once had huge tree relatives, but when the great swamps dried up long ago, the trees became extinct.

It is very tempting to take a string of club moss out of the woods, but in pulling up a part of the plant you rip off the roots and injure the entire plant. If the plant is an old one and has finished growing, it can't withstand being transplanted, and if it is young and still growing, it will be delicate and must have just the right soil and light conditions. The chances are the club moss will die quickly if you try to grow it at home, so it is better to leave it where you find it.

What are those small plants that seem to bear fancy candlesticks at the top?

They are clusters of the cones of the club moss *Lycopodium complanatum.* The cones, of less than one inch in length, grow in groups at the top of a single stalk. Within the cones are little capsules called sporangia.

Why does club moss have sporangia?

Sporangia are the little capsules or cases in which the spores are made, and they are found not only in club moss but in ferns, true mosses, and other plants that reproduce by spores. On the undersides of most ferns, for example, you will find brown spots, light green spots, or purplish dots. They look like the rivets in a ship's hull, or maybe like some kind of disease. They are part of the way a fern reproduces itself. The spots are called sori, and each one alone is called a sorus. A sorus has many parts that are too small for the eyes alone to see. Under a micro-

Lycopodium annotinum, the stiff club moss. Within the conelike structures are sporangia containing lots of powdery yellow spores.

The maidenhair fern, *Adiantum pedatum,* which grows in rich deciduous forest soils

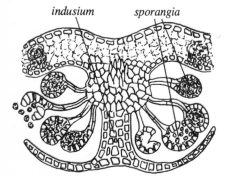

indusium   *sporangia*

Vertical or long section of a sorus

scope you would notice a tiny umbrella in the center of the sorus. It is called an indusium. Around the indusium ten to a hundred sporangia stand on small stalks.

Each tiny individual capsule, or sporangium, contains dozens of spores. Each spore can grow into a tiny, flat green plant. When the spores of the fern are ripe, the sporangium splits open, draws back, and hurls them into the air. A row of springy cells around the outside of the sporangium; called the annulus, makes this throwing action possible.

After the spores blow around a bit, they land. Millions of them were sent off from the fern, but only a few live. There has to be the right amount of water and the right amount of light for a spore to grow.

How can I tell if a plant is a fern?

Since no other plants have sori on the undersides of their leaves, one of the best ways to tell a fern is to see if you can find these clusters of sporangia.

On the grape fern the spore capsules are the size of pinheads and are not borne in clusters. Nor are they on the fern *Osmunda*, where the spore capsules are even smaller than

The underside of the leaflets of the maidenhair fern, showing the clusters of sporangia, called sori, where the spores are born

pinheads. But on most ferns you will find the sporangia ar-ranged on the underside of the leaves in rusty-brown groups—the sori—which you really can't miss. To identify ferns early in the growing season before the sori are present, or ferns on which such clusters never develop, you have to depend on pic-tures in books.

How does a fern get started in the ground?

The young fern gets started from a single spore, a tiny bit of fern matter consisting of a single cell as fine as dust. On the out-side of each spore is a thin waxy film coating called a cuticle.

A somewhat magnified view of the tiny one-cell-thick fern plant that results from a spore. It is here that the eggs and sperm are born.

Spores of ferns form very small plants that look totally unlike their parents. They are filmy green and one cell thick, and get started in shady, moist places wherever the spore happens to land. These tiny plants bear the eggs and sperm that unite to form the familiar plant again.

In conifers and flowering plants the egg-bearing part is hidden within the seed. The seeds of pines are in cones, and those of flowering plants are in pods or other fruits. In both cases the egg-bearing part is held protected as the seed develops within the parent plant. In ferns it grows separately. This is one reason why botanists say ferns and other spore-producing plants are more primitive then the conifers and flowering plants, because of the improvement or increase in protection of the reproductive body in the latter.

Is a fern frond a single leaf or many leaves?

It is a single leaf. Each little section along the frond is called a leaflet, or pinna. The pinnae are attached to the rachis, or midrib, of the leaf. On some ferns even the pinnae are divided into sections, and are called pinnules. The pinnules themselves may be further divided into pinnule-ules, and so on. If you look closely at the pinnae, you will see that they have a network of veins in them, and perhaps sori on the backside or along the edges underneath.

Some ferns are rather stiff, and some are soft and delicate. Why is that?

Stiff ferns have strong bundles of fibers running down the center of each leaf and its leaflets. The walls of the cells on the outside of the leaf may be especially thick and tough. If you

pinna

rachis

Frond

Fern fiddleheads. Each coil is a single leaf in the process of opening up in the spring.

snap open the rachis or midrib of a fern, you can see the tough bundles of fibers. If you bend a leaf of the Christmas fern, you can feel the hardness, you can also feel the waxy coating on the shiny leaflets. The hay-scented fern, on the other hand, has very delicate leaves with fewer fibers and thin-walled surface cells.

Was the fern I saw with a brown rusty region in the middle of the leaf sick?

No, it's not sick. The middle of the leaf is made up entirely of sporangia. Its name is the interrupted fern.

Fiddleheads in a slightly more advanced stage of development

How long have there been ferns?

Ferns very much like those you see in the forest now have been on earth for 350 million years or more. At that time, it was warm and very wet on Earth. Some of the ferns grew to be as large as trees. There are tree-sized ferns living today in tropical jungles, but many of the ferns and fernlike plants of that very early period have died out.

At the present time, in a single forest in the northeastern United States, you may find as many as two or three dozen different kinds of ferns.

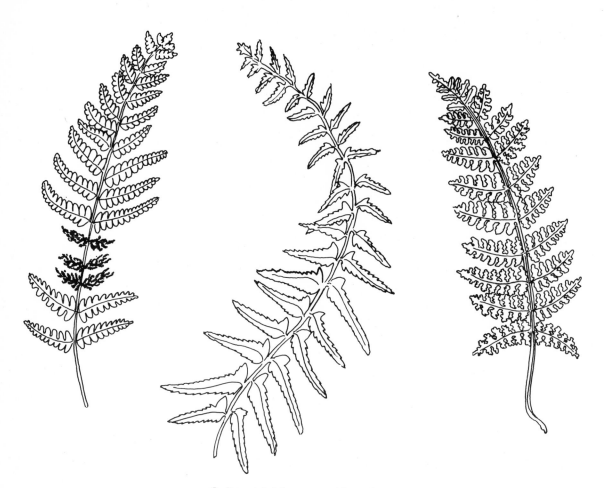

(Left to right) Interrupted fern, Christmas fern, and hay-scented fern

Where do baby moss plants come from?

Baby moss plants develop from spores, too, and the spores are made inside sporangia. When they are ready, they are thrown out of the capsule or just jostled out by the motion of the wind. Some of them land on ground that has the right amount of light and moisture to suit that particular moss species, and they begin to grow. Others land where it is too sunny or too shady or too wet or too dry or perhaps the kind of soil or rock on which they land is wrong for moss, and then the spores will die. When everything is suitable, the spores germinate and grow. The growth results in a fine thread of cells. Up from the threads come upright buds, which then turn into the upright plants that we know so well.

What good does moss do?

Moss keeps soil from washing away in a heavy rain. It collects soil particles in places where other plants cannot grow, such as on rocks. Moss can do this because, as we have seen, it is able to dry out when water is scarce and then become green again when wet.

Why does moss feel furry?

It feels furry because it is made up of thousands upon thousands of plants. These plants growing so close together form soft hairy mats of thin, fine leaves on flexible stems.

Are there different kinds of moss?

Yes, indeed. All moss may look alike at first glance, but if you examine several patches closely you will see that they are very different. The plants may differ in both color and size. In fact, if you look at them in detail, through a microscope, you will find that different species of moss are as unalike as oak and willow trees. Some of the leaves are arranged like feathers; some are extremely minute and tightly packed. Some moss leaves have simple shapes; others have elaborate ones.

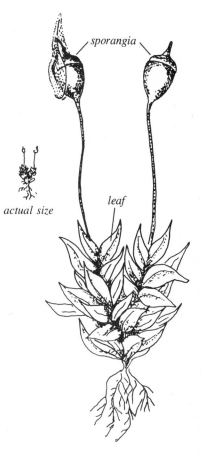

sporangia

actual size

leaf

Moss plant (enlarged)

How does moss stick to a rock?

Moss has tiny hairs called rhizoids at the bottom of each individual plant. These hairs are tough and grip the rough rock, so that the moss won't blow away. But it is easy for you or me to take a moss from a rock, and of course, when we do, we tear the little rhizoids.

Moss clings to rotting logs in the same way. Many kinds grow in damp swampy places, especially the more delicate forms that cannot stand bright sunlight.

Haircap moss, *Polytrichum,* one of the most common mosses

ANIMALS OF THE GROUND COVER

adult

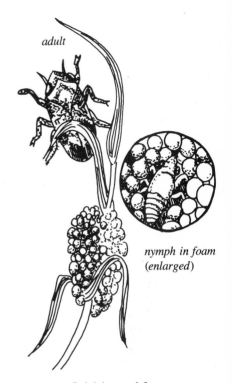

Why did that plant in the forest have a mound of foam on it?

That mound of foam was undoubtedly made by the nymph, or larva, of an insect called a spittlebug or froghopper. The nymph, which is about an eighth of an inch long, sucks a lot of juice out of tender plants and twigs, and blows some of it out in bubbles from its rear end. The bubbles keep the tiny insect damp and protect it somewhat from its enemies. But certain wasps dive right through the bubbles and grab the nymph out to eat it, so the bubbles do not serve as protection against all enemies.

nymph in foam (enlarged)

Spittlebug and foam

As I sat in the woods, an ant ran over my leg. Where does it live and how will it be able to find its way home?

If it was a common red ant, it probably lives in a big mound of earth somewhere near where you were sitting. Inside the mound, lots of tunnels and chambers have been carved out by the worker ants for the queen ant and her young. Another smaller kind of red ant that you might have seen lives in the ground, instead of in a mound. If the ant that ran up your leg was a large black one, it may very well have been a carpenter ant, whose nest is nearby in a rotted log or under a stone.

If the ant that ran over your leg had stopped for a moment to clean itself, you might have taken a closer look, and you would probably have seen two little antennae sticking out of its head. These are the ant's feelers, and they are really more important than its eyes. The end of each feeler has five very important joints. In some ants the first of these joints allows the ant to

Common black ant

know the smell of its own nest. Without it an ant might walk into the wrong ant hole, and be sorry—for the ants who lived there would probably attack the stranger. With the second joint an ant can tell if another ant was born from an egg of the same queen that gave birth to it. All ants from one queen are related. With the third joint an ant can tell its own smell, which it leaves on the ground, and can follow this smell back to the nest where it came from. The fourth and fifth joints tell an ant how to care for the young in the nest. Without all five joints an ant can't live as a member of a nest because it wouldn't know what it needs to know to do what it needs to do.

I heard a cricket in the woods. Does a cricket enjoy its own music?

No one knows if a cricket enjoys its music. It seems unlikely that a cricket has that kind of feeling. But the chirp of a cricket is an important way of passing on information in the forest. When a female cricket hears the song of a male cricket, she knows where to find a mate.

The sound is made by the male cricket rubbing one wing on top of the other. The female cricket hears the song with a little hearing box on the elbow of her foreleg. (There are deaf females in some species who find their mates by taste. But crickets who hear with their elbows are more common.) You can tell when you've found a female cricket because she has a long spine sticking out at the rear. This is her ovipositor, an egg-laying tool she uses to lay her eggs underground. When she is ready to lay her eggs, she simply pokes the ovipositor into the soil. The young, when they hatch from the eggs, look very much like adults but a lot smaller.

Field cricket

Tree cricket

What do crickets eat?

Wild crickets eat grain, herbs, fruit, and some dead meat. Pet crickets eat fruit and vegetables and perhaps a little sugar.

I found a snail in the forest. Don't snails live in water?

Mole cricket

Some do, but not all. If you look closely, you will find that there are lots of snails of several different kinds and sizes in the woods. Some are native American snails, snails whose ancestors have always been on this continent. Some are immigrant snails, whose ancestors stowed away on some leaves or roots being brought from another country. One snail that is doing very well in the northeastern woodlands came from England. Its name is *Cepea nemoralis*.

Forest snails breathe oxygen, as do all the snails that live in fresh water. Forest snails hide out in the daytime under leaves or on damp rocks—anywhere that affords some moisture. They creep about at night and eat fresh and rotting leaves and tiny webs of fungal threads called mycelium. For about six months in the winter, and in very dry weather in the summer, snails hibernate. For a snail, this means tucking itself into the ground somewhere and hiding in its shell, barely breathing.

Snails have spiral shells, and a "foot" and head that are joined together. When they creep along, a thin layer of mucus spreads on the ground as they slide across it. On the head end are two pairs of tentacles. The short pair is for smelling, and the long pair has simple eyes at the tips.

Every snail is both male and female, but a snail doesn't mate with itself. It slides up to another snail, and each one throws tiny stony darts into the other. The darts go right into their skin and stop somewhere inside. This gets the snails "excited," and

A common snail exploring a moist rock

Slug

they mate. They lay their eggs in the ground, and it takes the baby snails about a month to hatch out.

I saw a long shiny trail and a fleshy snail-like animal. What was it?

The shiny trail was made by a slug, who put down a coating of mucus to help it slide along through the forest. A slug is a snail that has either no shell at all or just a tiny piece of one deep inside its flesh. A slug lives much the same sort of life as a snail, and many of them don't do any particular harm. Certain kinds, though, do a lot of damage by eating up the young plants in gardens.

I hear there are little red lizards in the woods. Where should I look for them?

These little creatures are sometimes called lizards, but they are really a kind of salamander, and they are amphibian animals. Amphibians spend part of their lifetime in water and part on land. During the time they live in the water, they are dark brown with red spots, and they are called newts. But when they come out to live on land, they change in color to orange or red with yellow spots, and their name becomes red eft.

Red efts are beautiful little animals with fine silky skin. They have delicate legs with tiny feet ending in small pointed toes. Efts seem very fragile. But perhaps they are not as helpless as they look, for scientists say they have poison glands in their skin that make them bad-tasting to a lot of animals.

The red eft, *Dyemictelus*

You can pick up any efts you find, for whatever poison there is in their skin is not harmful to human beings. But it is hard to say where to look for them. They wander all over the woods for two or three years after they come on land and before they finally go back to the water. Try looking beside a rotted log, under a stone, or down among the ferns.

A warty toad hopped right across my path. Where was he going?

If it was in the spring, the toad you saw might have been on its way to a pond to find a mate. At any other time of the year it was probably just hunting around for food.

Every spring, after a winter of hibernation, toads return to water—the element from which they came—to mate and lay eggs. The male toads fertilize the eggs that the female toads lay in long strings in the water. One female makes thousands and thousands of eggs. The creatures that hatch out look nothing like toads. They swim around the water as tadpoles, eating and growing and gradually changing into tiny creatures with four legs and the look of a toad. The tadpoles stay in shallow water where they are less likely to be eaten by hungry fish, such as bass. When baby toads leave the water though, usually by the thousands, they are met by an army of hungry animals that eat them up as fast as they can. Birds, snakes, turtles, skunks, and many other creatures grab these tender little morsels of meat. Only a few tiny toads live to grow up—in spite of the mild poison in their skins.

The toad that you saw hopping through the woods may have been quite an old creature, perhaps even twenty or thirty years old. The wrinkled warty-looking skin of a toad has a much drier feel to it than a frog's skin. The toad's tough skin keeps water

Toad

in the toad's body and is good for life on land because it doesn't lose as much moisture to the air as does a frog's skin. A frog can't live long out of water because its skin has to be kept moist.

I found a turtle eating a fruit off a small plant. When I came closer, it shut itself inside its shell. What kind was it?

It was a box turtle, a land turtle that is becoming so scarce that some states have passed laws to protect it. The fruit it was

The eastern box turtle

A closeup view of the head of the box turtle

Hinged plastron

eating must have been a mayapple, a tender delicious fruit—to turtles—that grows on a plant whose leaves, stem, and roots are poisonous to people.

All turtles have two-part shells. The upper section is curved, and it is called a carapace; the bottom section is flat, and it is called a plastron. In most turtles the plastron is attached to the carapace in such a way that it can't move. But a box turtle has a hinged plastron and can shut its head, its tail, and its legs completely into the shell—unless, of course, the turtle has become too fat, in which case some fleshy part of it will not fit inside, but be left poking out at one end or the other. Turtles grow fat quite easily when they have plenty of berries, mayapples, insects, and earthworms to eat.

I had a chance to pick up a snake, but I didn't know if it would bite me. Would it have bitten me?

Almost any snake will try and bite you if you suddenly pick it up, but not all snakebites are dangerous. Make certain that any snake you corner or try to catch is not a poisonous one. Even after you have made sure that the snake you found is harmless, you should still be careful in the way you handle it. Hold it close behind its head, where it cannot bite you, because a snakebite can get infected. A poisonous snake will not attack you except in self-defense, so steer clear of any you encounter and give it a chance to get away.

Don't try and kill any snakes you see, for they do a very important job in the woods, eating rats and mice. Rats and mice will do a lot of damage if there get to be too many of them, for they eat birds' eggs, baby birds, the bark off trees, and lots of young plants. Snakes help to keep down the number of these animals. Occasionally snakes will eat birds' eggs and baby birds, but not in such large quantities as rats and mice do.

Have you ever tried to eat without your hands? It's not so hard if you are lapping something soft. But if you wanted to eat a steak and had no hands to use to cut it up, it would be a lot harder. A snake swallows its food whole—by the no-hands method. Unless it belongs to the constrictor family, there is no way for a snake to hold its food or to tear it up. Constrictors grasp their prey in the coils of their body, but if they let go of it even for a moment it will hop or squirm or run away. A snake has sharp teeth pointed down toward its stomach. Its mouth and jaws can stretch very wide, so that as a snake gulps its food, its mouth stretches out around it. The teeth keep it from getting back out, and the snake keeps gulping and stretching and swallowing until the food has disappeared. A few species of snakes kill their prey by squeezing it before they try to swallow it.

Copperhead

Timber rattler

Wood thrush

Rufous-sided towhee

I saw a bird hopping among the ferns. What was it?

Some birds nest on the ground and hunt their food among the small plants growing there. Others nest on the ground but go up into the branches of the middle layers to sing and hunt. Still others live in the middle layers or the canopy and come down to the ground to peck around for part of their food. So it is hard to say what sort of bird you saw, for there are many possibilities.

It might have been a wood thrush, looking for snails, spiders, and berries to eat. The wood thrush nests in low bushes. It builds a nest out of rootlets and dead leaves.

Or it could have ben a rufous-sided towhee. The towhee nests on the ground or in a low bush, but it hunts for insects and a few seeds among the dead leaves. While it's hunting, it kicks the leaves backward with both feet at once.

The ovenbird also builds its nest on the ground. Its nest is dome-shaped like an old-fashioned bread-baking oven and very carefully hidden. The ovenbird lines its little oven nest with grass and hair. It eats beetles, ants, bugs, and worms, and green caterpillars. Each pair of ovenbirds takes three to four acres of woods for its own domain and will not permit any other ovenbirds to live within its territory. The ovenbird has several different songs, one of which seems to say, "Teacher, teacher, teacher."

The black-and-white warbler is another bird that nests on the ground. It hops rapidly all over the forest floor, up and around the trunks of trees, and over and around their branches, looking for insects as it goes.

And if the woods you were in was a hemlock forest, what you may have seen was a hermit thrush or possibly a white-throated sparrow, who lives in coniferous forests and is a great eater of berries and seeds.

These are a few of the possibilities.

Something flew off the ground making a tremendous racket.
What was it?

It was probably a female pheasant. She made that loud noise
to startle you and catch your attention while her chicks scattered
into the woods. If you had waited, she might soon have landed
and wobbled on the ground as though she had an injured wing.
And if you had been a fox, you would probably have stalked
her, for she looks easy to catch. But she is not really an injured
bird, and if the fox tries to get near, she bursts into the air again
to lead it still farther away. When she has led it far from her
chicks, she will fly back to them and call them together. Then
they wander along through the woods in a little band, pecking
and probing for good things to eat—fat juicy insects, nice berries, tiny seeds, and little worms.

Black-and-white warbler

When I broke off a piece of an old stump, a little mouse ran out.
What kind was it?

It might very well have been a white-footed mouse, whose
other name is deer mouse. It is called white-footed because it
has white underneath and on its four paws; it is called deer
mouse because of its large ears. This little mouse has huge eyes,
and a tail that is as long as the rest of it. Perhaps you scared it
out of its nest in the stump, where it was sleeping with its
babies. A female has a litter about three times every summer.

During the day the white-footed mouse sleeps. It stirs about

Pheasants

at night looking for tiny seeds, fruits, and insects. It is an important animal in the woods because of its liking for insects. Some of the insects it hunts hurt trees. Of course it doesn't realize the importance of its job—it simply likes that kind of insect. This mouse is in turn hunted by prowling meat-eating animals, such as foxes and owls and snakes.

White-footed mice

I saw a chipmunk run inside a stone wall. Does it live there?

A chipmunk may have an entrance tunnel to its burrow through the stone wall, but it probably lives down in the ground under the wall, or next to it, in a series of tunnels and hollows and storerooms. A chipmunk needs a place to make a nest for its young, a lot of space to store quarts of seeds and nuts and grains, and entranceways and escape tunnels.

The chipmunk finds a good part of its food on the ground and is mostly a vegetarian. But once in a while, one will climb a tree and eat an egg or a nestling bird. As a chipmunk goes busily about gathering food, it has to keep a sharp lookout for its enemies, the meat eaters—hawks, snakes, and foxes.

Eastern chipmunk

I smelled a skunk when I was in the woods, but I couldn't see it. Where was it?

If you smelled a skunk during the day, you were probably smelling the plant, skunk cabbage. Perhaps you broke off a part of the plant without realizing it. A skunk sleeps during the day and comes out of its hole at night to hunt.

But if the odor continued and was very strong, you may have smelled a skunk defending itself from an enemy—perhaps a dog or fox that found it asleep in its hole. The scent drifts along on the wind. A skunk is a very clean animal, and it doesn't smell at all unless it has just used the scent glands at the base of its tail to spray some of its terrible perfume.

At night the skunk pads around through the woods in a flat-footed way. It goes slowly, not much worried about danger because of its spray, which animals hate the smell of. It snoops and pokes about for insects and the nests of mice. It tears into the ground or claws open rotten logs. If it smells mice, it digs them out with its long, straight claws. Sometimes it eats turtle eggs, which it finds buried near a stream. Skunks eat huge numbers of insects every day and lots of mice.

Striped skunk

What do deer eat?

In the summer, deer eat grass and small plants. And in the winter, when the grass is dead and plants are, too, they eat tender twigs and the bark from young trees. A deer has no front teeth in its upper jaw, so it has to use its tongue and its lower teeth to tear loose its food.

Deer are animals that chew their cuds the way cows do. Sometimes you see them lying in the forest, chewing without ever taking a new bite. When they do that, they are grinding up the food they swallowed earlier that day.

As a deer plucks off grass, it doesn't chew but swallows it and stores it in the first part of its four-part stomach. The plants get damp there, and bacteria start breaking down the cellulose plant walls. After the food is softened, it is shaped into lumps called cuds. When a deer gets a chance to stay still for a while, it burps up a lump of cud and goes to work on it, grinding it down on its big flat teeth—the molars. When the cud is in small enough pieces and mixed with plenty of spit, the deer again swallows it. It goes to a different part of the stomach this time. The rest of the deer's stomach and its intestine finish off diges-

White-tailed deer

tion. Deer get everything from the plant food that they need to grow and stay healthy.

Deer are often pictured with antlers, and you might surprise such a deer in the woods, and have a chance to see antlers on a living animal. Only male deer have antlers, which are living bone and have blood circulating in them. They start to grow each year in the early spring, about two weeks after the old antlers have fallen off. It is rare to find a set of antlers lying on the forest floor because deer and other animals eat them. The antlers are full of calcium, a mineral that animals need.

I saw a fox that didn't seem to be afraid of me. Could I have tried to pet it?

No, it is best never to go near a furry wild animal that is acting strangely unafraid. It is not natural for a fox to be tame, unless it has been raised by hand by someone and lives on an animal farm. Out in the woods a fox that is wandering fearlessly near you may have rabies—a very serious disease. You could catch the disease if the fox bit or scratched you. The same thing would hold true for a raccoon or a skunk—never trust it if it doesn't act wild. And when you leave the forest, tell someone about the behavior of the animal you saw.

Most foxes stay hidden during the day and come out at night to hunt. Some live in holes that other animals have dug and deserted, but other foxes dig hideouts for themselves. Some of the dens have several entrances and exits.

A fox eats many animals that are pests to people, such as mice and rats and rabbits. Sometimes a fox will eat a few bird eggs or baby birds, but it eats so few of these compared to the number of mice and rats that a fox can be said to do less harm than good.

Red fox

Many of the animals that a fox eats are part of a group of animals of which there are just too many. Some years there are just too many rabbits. They need places to hide and plenty of food, but since there are too many of them, all the good burrows get taken. Some of the rabbits are left without good places to hide. The strongest, quickest rabbits also find and eat up most of the best food, and some rabbits grow weak from hunger. The wandering rabbits, who can't find good hiding places, and the weak rabbits, who are not getting enough of the right food, are the ones that are easiest for foxes to catch. So a lot of what foxes eat comes from the population explosions of certain kinds of animals.

Foxes don't only eat mice and rabbits. They also like fish, crayfish, fruit, and surprisingly, grass.

Do raccoons always wash their food?

No. It seems that raccoons only wash their food when water is handy. If they are in the middle of the woods and nowhere near a wet place, they eat whatever food they have caught anyhow. When they do wash it, they dunk it in and out of the water carefully, but they never seem to look to see if it is really clean. Some zoologists think that raccoons are trying to wash out the poisons from the skin of one of their favorite foods—a toad. Another theory is they are trying to get rid of grit, for raccoons also eat earthworms, frogs, newts, insects, and all kinds of small animals, some of which are likely to be gritty. To top it off, raccoons like berries and nuts, too. In fact, they eat just about anything that is edible.

Raccoons come out at night to hunt, and they are able to hunt in many different kinds of places. They can climb trees; they can swim; and they can dig.

Raccoon

5 The Soil

What is the soil?

Beneath the dimly lit plant and animal communities of the ground cover lies the deepest layer of the forest—the soil. The soil is the place where the roots of all the large trees and almost all the smaller plants take anchor. The soil is the home base for plants, yet without plants to hold it down, the soil would not exist. The earth would be barren rock, for if there were no plants, both wind and water would carry away the soil, depositing it in the seas or lakes.

Soil is made up of many substances. Its topmost layer is called litter, which consists of dead leaves, logs, branches, seeds, and other parts of dead plants, as well as dead animals. Underneath the litter is a layer of stuff that is decomposing—that is, losing its own form and turning into soil. It is called raw humus, because it is only partially broken down. Beneath the

Three *Russula* mushrooms

Layers of the soil

raw humus is the real humus, the part of the soil that is rich in the mineral nutrients all plants need to grow. The real humus is often black, and you can't find anything in it that looks like leaves or branches or the bodies of animals because they have been so much changed. These top three layers of the soil are called the A horizon by scientists.

Underneath the A horizon are layers of silt, sand, and clay, along with small stones that are in the process of breaking down into soil particles, and below this are layers of larger rocks surrounded by more silt, sand, and clay. These two layers are called the B and C horizons or rock horizons.

In the soil live all sorts of animals, from tiny protozoans, springtails, and mites to larger creatures such as earthworms, shrews, and woodchucks. Soil is much more than broken-up particles of rock and decayed plants and animals. It, too, is a thriving community of living things.

Does all the dead stuff do any good while it's on the forest floor?

Although it may not look so, the dead and decaying litter on the forest floor provides food for many creatures. The dead branches, seeds, logs, and leaves, the dead animals of all kinds, are certainly not your sort of food nor mine, but they are food for fungi, bacteria, slime molds, and various kinds of soil animals—springtails, mites, protozoans, millipedes, earthworms, and others. Until these bits of dead plant and animal matter are broken down into simpler chemical elements, they still contain some of the energy of the sunlight in which they once grew.

The energy of the sunlight is held in the molecules that make up the litter, the cellulose molecules of plant cell walls and the proteins of animal muscles, for example. When these are broken down by decay on the forest floor, the energy is gradually released into the air as heat. At the same time the important mineral nutrients of which the litter was made—nitrate, phosphate, sulfate, calcium, and magnesium—are returned to the water in the soil. The nutrients will enter new plants through the roots, and again become a part of the structure of plant cells. When these same plants are eaten by animals, the minerals will become part of the structure of the animal's body, and so on. Without the decomposers, the litter in the forest would pile up in a great heap, and the mineral nutrients needed by plants and animals for survival could never be used.

Litter in a deciduous forest

How does a leaf get broken down?

A leaf that has fallen off a tree or a smaller plant dies as it lies on the ground. It gets wet from the rain, and soon microscopic organisms—bacteria, fungi, protozoans, and slime molds—start to work on it. At the same time larger creatures attack the leaf. Among the first are the little springtails, which chew small holes in the outside layers of the leaf. More holes are chewed by the larvae of small flies. Then other animals arrive—snails and slugs, millipedes and earwigs, woodlice, and the larvae of larger flies. All of them chew bits out of the leaf until it looks like a net. Veins and bits of leaf are sometimes left here and there, but the leaf is full of holes. If the leaf stays damp, the bacteria continue to live on it and to break it down, and small relatives of earthworms as well as tiny springtails and beetle mites go on with the chewing. At any time a big earthworm may come along and take what is left down into its burrow to eat. What was once a leaf will then have disappeared entirely.

Earwig

How long does it take for a leaf to disappear?

It takes several years for a leaf, such as an oak leaf, to turn back into carbon dioxide, water, nitrate, phosphate, sulfate, calcium, magnesium, iron, and all the rest of the chemicals that it is made of.

Why does it smell funny when I dig under dead leaves?

The funny smell is the smell of the products given off by bacteria and fungi. There are really two ways of looking at this. Some of the odor is actually made by the tiny organisms themselves. For example, there are strands of fungi and actinomycetes—threadlike bacteria—going all through the grounds, and when you dig, you break some of them. Then they give off their chemical odors, which waft to your nose. Some of the odor comes from the materials these microorganisms are breaking down. As they cause the decay of a dead leaf or animal, certain odors are released—the smell of ammonia and the stench of hydrogen sulfide are examples.

What sorts of things grow on rotting logs and what makes logs rot?

As with leaves and branches, when a whole tree falls, the trunk begins to rot. Among the first things you are likely to see growing on it are slime molds and fungi—especially jelly fungi and mushrooms—all of which help to rot the log. If you strip off a piece of the bark from such a log, you will find those long stringlike cables known as rhizomorphs underneath, and if you were to keep peeling them away, you would soon have enough to wrap around yourself several times.

A rhizomorph is made of slender cables of fungus, like strands of very thin spaghetti, lying next to each other and

A rotting tree stump

A jelly fungus growing on a rotting log. This variety is a bright orange color.

bound together by a sheath. They are often found under the bark of rotting logs and stumps. Fungal rhizomorphs secrete enzymes—certain kinds of chemicals—which digest the wood and then take it in as food. After a while the bark gets loose, and long sections of it begin to fall off. Dead leaves fall and catch in rough places on the log. Sticking there, they begin to turn into soil. Moss spreads itself over the log, and flowering plants, ferns, and young trees begin to grow on top, sinking their roots into the wood and loosening it up even more. Ants dig tunnels in the wood under the loose bark. Millipedes start to munch on it, and pillbugs and other insects move into the softening wood. It may take more than one hundred years, but eventually these fallen trees become soil.

Cedar wood and chestnut wood are highly water-repellent and take an extra long time to rot. In fact all the hardwoods take a long time—woods like oak and walnut. The softwoods, such as pine, rot a good deal faster. In some forests you see trees that came down in the 1938 hurricane that have still not rotted completely. The speed of decay depends a lot on how much moisture gets into the wood, helping the fungi and other decay organisms to grow.

Do all rotting logs have the same things growing on them?

No, they don't. What grows nicely on one rotting log may not grow well on another kind. For example, orange, white, and black jelly fungi all grow on different kinds of wood. Some woods have natural chemicals in them that keep any fungi from growing on them.

Bracket fungi growing on a decaying log

An old tree trunk of the American chestnut. The tree died forty to fifty years ago in the great chestnut blight, but because the wood is very durable, the trunk takes a long time to rot.

THE VARIETIES OF FUNGI

What are fungi, and what do they do?

Fungi are threadlike organisms that get the food they need by secreting enzymes that break down dead materials. Fungi absorb the food right through the walls of their cells. Although the parts of them that you can see you find among the plants of the ground cover, fungi are a basic part of the life process of the soil. They are the most important decomposers in the forest.

But fungi do far more than break down dead materials. Among the fungi in the forest are the yeasts, small round cells which can land in the sugary material of a rotting fruit and cause it to ferment, making alcohol. In fact there are a number of very important fungi that cause fermentation and are used for the manufacture of chemicals in factories. Fungi are also used in making antibiotics, such as penicillin, and in making cheese, such as blue cheese.

Some fungi form fruiting bodies, which are the parts you notice as you walk through the woods. The cap and stalk of the mushroom, the ball of the puffball, the coral-like branches of the coral fungus, are all fruiting bodies.

How many kinds of fungi are there?

There are thousands of different kinds of fungi. Some of them are so small that you can't see them, though you can smell them when you disturb the soil. Some of them are large and tough, almost like pieces of wood, and some are soft and very fragile. Botanists divide the fungi into three main groups, with one additional group as well.

First is the group of algal fungi, consisting of threads of cells.

They are called Phycomycetes and some of them cause serious plant diseases. The powdery mildew that destroys grape leaves is one of the diseases. Another Phycomycete brought about the terrible potato blight in Ireland over 100 years ago, which caused two million people to leave Ireland and another million to starve.

The next group of fungi are the Ascomycetes, or sac fungi. Often these grow in the shape of little cups, or urns. Their masses of threads are everywhere in the woods. The spores are shot out of little sacs called asci. Yeasts are Ascomycetes, and there are many different kinds in the woods. The edible morel is also an ascomycete fungus.

The third group of fungi are the Basidiomycetes, or club fungi. In this group, or closely related to it, are the smuts, the rusts (such as the pine-blister rust), jelly fungi, mushrooms, puffballs, and stinkhorns. Of all the fungi in the woods these are the most noticeable.

Clitocybe illudens, a mushroom known as the lantern fungus. Bright orange in color, it has gills that shine in the dark.

The remaining odd group, which biologists are not sure are fungi at all, are the beautiful slime molds or Myxomycetes. These living things are partly like the microscopic animals known as amoebae and partly like fungi. They creep around rotting logs and leaves, but later, like fungi, form spore-bearing stalks, which are often very beautiful.

Why are fungi never green?

Fungi are never green because they have no chlorophyll in them. They don't need it either, because they don't use the energy of sunlight to make food. Fungi as a group absorb their food.

Scientists have discovered that some fungi are sensitive to light, even though they do not use it to make food. They are also sensitive to gravity, "knowing" how to oppose it by growing straight up. That is why a mushroom popping horizontally out of the side of a tree will soon turn upright. This is known as negative geotropism.

What do I see? A mushroom! Where did it come from?

After a rainstorm, a conifer or a broadleaf forest can often surprise you because suddenly mushrooms have sprung up all around. They have been ready in the soil for some time, waiting for the earth to get damp enough for them to grow.

Most mushrooms in the forest look different from the ones you buy in a grocery store or supermarket. They come up in many different colors and sizes, popping out of the insides of logs, from under dead leaves, or through a web of pine needles. Their umbrellas spread out wide and are flat or nicely curved. But you can always tell a mushroom for they all have the same basic shape: a stalk with an umbrella cap, and gills like the spokes of a wheel underneath the cap.

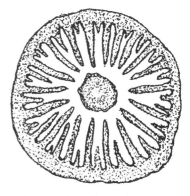

Cross section of a mushroom cap

Why do some mushrooms poison you?

A mushroom has nothing against you personally. Some mushrooms are poisonous because they have chemical substances called alkaloids in them that attack the human nervous system and paralyze it. Some mushrooms are so poisonous that they kill anyone who eats them—usually a small bite will do it. Others are mildly poisonous for some people, and not poisonous

Amanita muscaria, the fly amanita, one of the deadly mushrooms

at all for others. It's only sensible never to pick or eat mushrooms in the woods, unless you are accompanied by an expert who can identify them.

What were the beautiful things I found growing on the forest floor? They looked like coral and broke off so easily.

You are undoubtedly looking at some Clavarias, or coral fungi. They come in a wide range of colors. Usually they are all yellow or cream-colored, but sometimes they are bright yellow or violet. Coral fungi spring out of the ground and very soon after begin to give off spores. Deer, rodents, birds, and insects will all be after the coral fungi as soon as they come up, for they are very good to eat.

Another beautiful fungus is the dog's-tooth fungus. You may find it growing out of the side of a tree. The part you see, which may be as big as a child's head, is the fruiting body of the

Two species of *Clavaria,* or coral fungi

An edible morel, *Morchella esculenta,* which grows to be about 4 to 6 inches high

fungus. The rest consists of threads inside the tree. It has millions of spores on the inside of its teeth.

What was the reason for the hollow space and the brainlike foldings in the fungus I found?

You must have been looking at the edible morel, a fungus of the genus *Morchella*. No one can say why it is hollow. But the ins and outs of its folded sides are covered with thousands of the little tubular sacs called asci, which carry spores in groups of eight. Inside a morel that is old and overripe, you will find slugs and maggots. They are using it for food. Some kinds of morels are delicious to eat. Other fungi that look like morels, such as the saddle fungus, will make you good and sick if you try eating them.

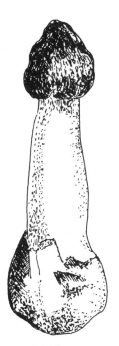

Stinkhorn

I saw a strange fungus that smelled odd. What was it?

It was a stinkhorn, *Phallus impudicus*. If you had leaned close to it, you would have found out that its name fits it very well. Most people dislike the smell, but flies don't seem to mind it at all. They come swarming to the plant and eat bits of it. Often they swallow spores, which on some stinkhorns are all over the surface and on others are down in a little net around the stalk. The spores pass through the flies' stomachs and come out in the fly specks. If the speck is dropped in a good place for the spore to grow, you will eventually find another stinkhorn there.

There is no beating the stinkhorn once it starts to grow. It changes from a small round egg to a big upright fungus in about five hours. Then its fat tip, the gleba, starts to become liquid and turns sticky and horrid-smelling. Sometimes the tip turns a greenish color. Yet this strange fungus has a certain beauty.

A small round ball sent out a cloud of dust when I kicked it. What was it?

It was a puffball fungus. When puffballs are ripe, they are packed with millions and sometimes billions of spores, each one so small it can only be seen with the help of a microscope. The spores are hidden inside the leathery skin of the puffball until something disturbs it. Then out they come as a cloud of brown dust.

Before the puffball gets ripe, the inside of it is a pure creamy white. Some puffballs are very good to eat, but to choose those that are you need to get the advice of someone who knows them well. Some puffballs grow to be the size of a pumpkin—a large one; others stay the size of a pea. One as small as your fist can have enough spores in it to cover the whole state of Massachusetts with puffballs, if they all managed to grow.

A puffball fungus

Geaster, the earth star, one of the puffballs

Is the Indian pipe a fungus?

An Indian pipe looks something like a fungus because it's so pale, but it's really a flowering plant. The Indian pipe, *Monotropa,* has leaves that are white. It has no pigments, either to give it color or to capture light. It might as well have no leaves at all because it makes no use of them. And yet it is still able to live because it gets its food in an unusual way. The roots of the Indian pipe are branched and look like coral. They are covered all over with a fine net of fungal threads. These threads spread away from the roots of the Indian pipe through the soil to the roots of a spruce or pine tree. They form another net around the stubby, branched roots of the tree. You might think it bad for the tree to have its roots so well wrapped up in fungus, but it's not. The tree can't grow well without the help of the fungus.

The fungus frees minerals from the soil, which are taken in

Indian pipes, *Monotropa uniflora*

by the roots of both the Indian pipe and the tree. Thus the tree gets some of the food it needs. Like all trees the pine or spruce tree makes sugar in its leaves. Some of that sugar is sent down into the roots of the tree. From the roots it crosses the fungal bridge and goes into the Indian-pipe plant. Scientists have done tests that show that it takes only a few hours for a molecule of sugar to move from the tree into the Indian pipe. The Indian pipe grows well and quickly on the meal made for it by the tree (and on the minerals that it also gets from the fungus). An Indian pipe reaches full flower in just about a week after springing up under the pine needles. It is thought that the fungus that joins the roots of the tree with the roots of the Indian pipe is a kind of fungus known as *Boletus*.

ROOTS

What do the roots of trees do underground?

Besides holding the tree in place as it grows higher and higher, roots probing between the rocks deep under the ground find water to send up to the branches and leaves. Tiny hairs on the roots sort out the minerals in the soil, and send the growing, working parts of the tree just what they need. Here are the names of some of the mineral nutrients that roots must have from the soil in order to live: iron, magnesium, calcium, zinc, manganese, copper, potassium, phosphate, and sulfate. The roots of many trees go deep underground. The part that you see in the forest is really only a section of the whole plant.

The roots of smaller soft-stemmed plants serve the same purpose as the roots of trees: they anchor the plant and provide it with water and minerals.

Large buttress roots. Common to many trees, they prop up the tree.

*Are the roots of trees and soft-stemmed flowering plants differ-
ent from each other?*

Yes, they are. The soft-stemmed plants have very little wood
in their stems and roots. Their roots are never as big as the roots
of trees. The roots of many small plants die each fall with the
plant, though some live over the winter to produce new leaves
and flowers in the spring.

Trees are plants with a great deal of wood in their stems,
limbs, and roots. A new ring of wood forms in the root each
year just as it does in the tree trunk. Some trees, such as the
dogwood, have extremely tough roots, but the roots of most
trees are not as stiff as their stems.

Why are roots twisted and hairy?

Roots are twisted because as they grow they change direction
underground, moving between pebbles, rocks, and boulders. If
a root could not change direction, its way would soon be
blocked.

Roots never stop growing while the plant is alive. They grow
at the tip, and they get fatter around. Like the trunk, they also
have bark.

To do their work, which is to take water and minerals for the
plant out of the ground, roots have billions of tiny hairs on
them, which twist and wind among the tiniest particles of soil.
Roots are even more hairy than those you are used to seeing, for
when you rip up a plant to look at its roots, you leave all the really fine hairs behind in the dirt.

How does a root know to grow down?

Scientists do not yet know why a root grows toward the earth.

If you take a straight root and lay it on top of the ground, the root will turn its tip toward the ground. If you turn a plant upside down, the root will turn around and begin to grow down. Scientists call this positive geotropism. This means attraction toward the earth.

What does a root look like inside?

If you cut a root straight across and look at the place you cut, you will see that a root looks a lot like a stem inside. You will not be able to see much more than that without a microscope.

But if you were to look at a thin section of a root through a microscope, you would find that the cells of the root form a pattern. On the outside of the root are the cells of the epidermis, or skin. Some of these cells grow out from the epidermis into slender hairs. Just underneath is a layer of spongy cells, called the cortex. There are spaces between the cells of the spongy layer that are filled with gases, such as carbon dioxide and sometimes nitrogen. Next comes a tight layer of cells with no air spaces at all between them. This layer surrounds the xylem cells that carry water and the phloem cells that carry both water and food.

Vertical or long section of a root tip

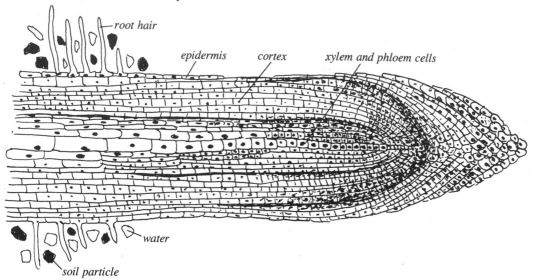

ANIMALS OF THE SOIL

Are there many animals living in the soil?

If you examined even a little cube of soil, no bigger than three inches on each side, you would find more small animals in it than you could count. In fact there are so many that the number can only be estimated. Opposite is a list of the animals calculated by soil scientists to be in a three-inch cube of soil in a rich broadleaf forest. And besides these, there are countless millions of microscopic plants—bacteria, fungi, actinomycetes, and slime molds.

Microscopic views of a nematode (left) and a soil mite

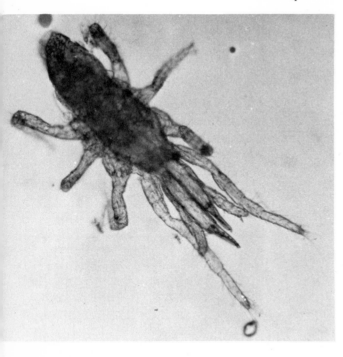
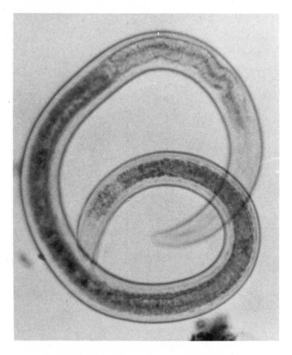

A microscopic view of a springtail

NAME OF ORGANISM	SIZE	AMOUNT
Protozoans	Microscopic	1,000,000
Tardigrades and rotifers	Microscopic	500
Nematodes	Pinhead	30,000
Mites	Pinhead	2,000
Springtails	Pinhead	1,000
Spiders, crustaceans, millipedes, and insects	Pinhead to pea-sized	100
Enchytraeid worms	Pinhead to pea-sized	50
Earthworms	Up to ten or more inches	2

What were the little white, fleshy, jointed things I found when I dug in the woods?

Some of them were larvae, the wormlike creatures that hatch from the eggs of different kinds of insects. Many of them live in the ground for a while before they pupate and change into their adult forms.

Beetle larvae eat earthworms, snails, slugs, and insects. Sexton-beetle larvae eat dead animals. The larvae of other insects, such as flies, eat leaves or the roots of grass and other plants.

The Japanese beetle lives in the ground, and so does the larva of the fat brown June bug, another kind of beetle. The June-bug larva lives in the soil for three years, eating plant roots and other kinds of vegetable food. The larva, which hatches from an egg, grows and grows in the soil. Finally it makes a perfect little case for itself. Inside that case, called a pupa, it changes into an adult beetle. You can tell a beetle from other insects by its hard outside wings, which cover a pair of transparent wings underneath.

Some of these larvae do a lot of damage to the plants they eat and some do not.

What were the fat worms I found in a rotting log?

They were probably not worms at all, but the larval stages of one kind of beetle or another. They live and grow in the log until they are ready to turn into their adult forms.

What was the slimy stuff I found on a rotting log?

What you probably found was a slime mold, which is a strange kind of organism. A slime mold is made up of millions

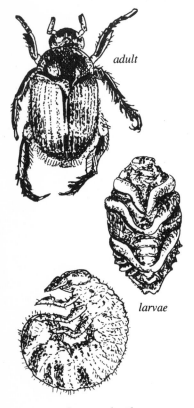

adult

larvae

Japanese beetle

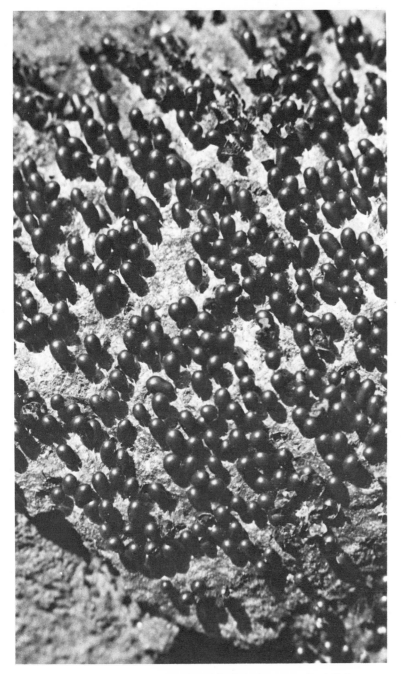

A slightly magnified view of a slime mold in the spore stage. Each little capsule, smaller than a pinhead, contains hundreds of spores.

of individual microscopic cells that band together into a slime mass called a plasmodium. A slime mold can move itself along, and as it moves, it eats, taking in small bits of rotting log as well as tiny pieces of leaf and bacteria. These particles are its food, and some botanists say that a plasmodium can digest something as big as a mushroom if it happens to move over it. The slime mold helps in the business of turning dead leaves and rotting wood back into raw chemicals the plants can use.

A slime mold lives in shady places and oozes away from strong light. It moves toward moisture and the taste of food. If the woods become very dry, the slime mold may either dry up on the spot in a thin crust or it may change completely and go into a spore stage. In that case it puts up stalks with capsules on them that are like miniature fungi. The capsules are filled with spores that turn into swimming creatures—tiny cells with whip-like swimming hairs—when the woods are damp again. When these little swimmers join together, they lose their hairs and turn into a plasmodium again.

coiled

walking

Millipedes

What is the name of the little animal covered with armor plate, the one that has so many legs and rolls up into a ball?

Its name is millipede, and it rolls up into a ball to protect itself when you touch it. It can also protect itself by letting off a very powerful, unpleasant smell from its stink glands. You will find it crawling in and out of the litter on the forest floor. The tough outside covering, or armor plate, is the skeleton of the animal. It is made hard by lime salts. All the soft parts of the millipede are inside.

When the millipede thinks the coast is clear, it will unroll itself and stretch out. Then you can see its many sections, or segments. Most of the segments have two pairs of jointed legs.

They are moved in a smooth motion by muscles found under its armor, all along the sides of the animal, from front to back. The millipede seems to glide along, as the ripple of leg movement goes from head end to rear.

A millipede has antennae to feel things, simple eyes, and jaws for chewing up dead plants and leaves. It helps in the process of turning litter back into soil. When a millipede has eaten for a time, its soft parts become so crowded inside its armor plate that the tough outside covering is forced to yield. Getting rid of the too tight suit of armor plate is called shedding. Once the skeleton splits open and drops off, the skin underneath expands and then hardens into a new, bigger armor plate, or exoskeleton.

I saw a little animal with many, many legs. What was it?

If it was flat, as well as small, and had lots of legs, but fewer than a millipede, and looked something like a cross between a millipede and a spider—you probably saw a centipede. Did you get a close enough look to see if its body was divided into sections, and whether each section had a pair of legs—that is, one leg on each side of each section? Did the animal waggle its whole body from side to side as it moved along? If all these things were so, and if it had a kind of rounded head that was easily seen, you were definitely looking at a centipede. Next time you see one, though, watch out! A centipede bites, and its bite hurts. The first pair of legs has been changed, through evolution, into a pair of poison fangs. They have changed from something to walk on to something to sting with. This was a big change, one that took thousands, perhaps millions, of years to come about.

Centipedes live under the leaves on the forest floor and in

Centipede

crumbling wood under the bark of old rotted logs. But they are not the least bit interested in eating the plant material they live in; they like meat. They hunt many of the plant-eating animals that you find in the forest soil—insects, earthworms, and slugs, among others. They sometimes even eat each other.

Where do you find earthworms in the forest?

It's easiest to find earthworms in the soil of a broadleaf forest. Just dig under the litter into the humus. There are fewer worms in a pine or spruce forest, where the soil is acid and the calcium they need is scarce.

Earthworms make the soil more porous by boring tunnels from the surface of the ground to as much as a yard or more underground. These tunnels are good for the soil, for they let air and water into it. Earthworms seem to be comfortable only when they have the walls of their tunnels fitting snugly against their sides. To move forward through the soil, earthworms jam their bristles in and out to secure a hold or to let go.

Earthworms have the camouflage color of the soil, but their color does not protect them from sunlight. Certain rays of the sun—those known as ultraviolet—can kill earthworms quickly. That is why you see earthworms moving around restlessly when they get into the light. They can't see the light because they have no eyes, but they can feel it. They can also feel the vibrations of your footsteps on the ground.

Why is an earthworm gritty inside?

An earthworm is gritty inside, because it is full of dirt, as well as the pieces of leaves and other parts of plants that it eats. It takes in these things and grinds them between small stones in its crop. With the help of bacteria in its gut, it gets the nutrients it needs from the soil and dead plants. The stuff it can't use is expelled as castings and left above ground. If you look closely among the leaves, you will see many of these in little piles.

The clayey humus of the castings is held together by mucus from the gut of the earthworm. Because the mucus is a good place for bacteria to live and multiply, an earthworm is valuable in another way: it unwittingly helps to increase the number of soil bacteria, which in turn help to do the final job of turning plant material into soil.

A common earthworm poking about in the forest litter

How does an earthworm breathe underground?

It breathes by soaking up oxygen from the water in the soil through its damp skin. But if there is too much moisture in the soil—during a rainstorm, for example—the earthworm is really in a pickle. The rain comes pouring into its tunnels, and if the water doesn't have enough oxygen, the worm will drown. An earthworm heads for the top of the forest floor when its tunnels are flooded. Then all is well unless it gets too much sunshine, which contains ultraviolet rays that are harmful to it.

I found a dead animal that looked like a very small mouse, but its nose was longer than a mouse's. What kind of animal was it?

It may have been a shrew, one of the tiniest of mammals. This furry little creature measures two or three inches in length. It has warm blood, and the female nurses its young just as larger mammals do. There is one variety of shrew—the pygmy shrew—that weighs no more than a dime.

A shrew is tough and fearless in its own world, but if you caught one and took it home, you would have a hard time keeping it alive. It is a nervous animal, and in a few hours would probably die of fright. If it didn't die of fright, it might die of hunger a little later. A shrew is said to need to eat day and night to stay alive, taking off only a few hours here and there for naps.

At night the shrew comes out into the forest to hunt, leaving its underground tunnels where it has been hunting and sleeping during the day. It is constantly looking for food, especially for meat—insect meat. This makes the shrew an important inhabitant of the forest community, because it likes to eat many insects that attack trees. It likes other food, too, and hunts for snails and slugs, dead animals, nuts, and berries. It will even at-

Common shrew

tack a mouse if it falls into one of its tunnels. A shrew has weak eyes, so it hunts mostly with its nose. Some shrews are poisonous. Watch out! Don't get nipped.

What are those soft winding bumps in the ground?

They are mole tunnels made by the tiny gray mole as it burrows through the ground. The ones that you feel under your feet as you walk are the more quickly made mole tunnels. They are not designed to last. Deep underground are a set of permanent tunnels that can't be crushed by your footsteps. They lead to a small fortress under a wall or the roots of a tree. A mole has very tiny eyes, and can scarcely tell day from night, but it doesn't really need eyes at all in its pitch-black tunnels. It has a very sensitive nose and smells its food. It also has a sensitive tail for feeling its way when it backs up. A mole has extra-strong paws for digging and forty-four very sharp teeth. As it burrows, it eats earthworms, insects, seeds, bulbs, and roots. A hard worker, a mole needs a good deal to eat. There are no lazy moles.

One variety of mole is very curious-looking; it has tentacles all over its nose that wiggle in all directions. This mole sometimes takes a swim or runs about on top of the snow. It is called the star-nosed mole and is quite comical in appearance.

Common and star-nosed moles

What kind of animal digs a big hole in the ground?

Big holes in the ground are often made by woodchucks. In the summer they like to live in the fields and have their burrows there. But in the winter they sleep in burrows in the woods. Woodchucks are great tunnelers. They may dig down as much as twenty to forty feet underground. They patiently dig right through all the horizons—the litter and the humus and the rock

Woodchuck

horizons. In the middle of one of the tunnels the woodchuck makes a cozy, grassy nest. Every woodchuck has escape tunnels, leading out of the burrow in several directions. And there is at least one plunge hole—a hole that goes straight down into the ground with no pile of dirt outside it to show another animal where it is. A woodchuck can take a dive down its plunge hole and disappear in a moment into its tunnels.

Woodchucks have another name that most people know; they are also called groundhogs. Every February second, according to folk belief, the groundhog comes out of its burrow from deep winter sleep. If the sun is shining and it sees its shadow, it returns to its burrow and goes back to sleep. This means winter will last six weeks longer. If it's cloudy, and the groundhog is unable to see its shadow, it remains above ground, thus predicting an early end to winter. In fact, groundhogs often sleep right through the date, so soundly do they sleep when they hibernate. One naturalist writes that he dug up a hibernating groundhog and rolled it around on the ground and that it kept right on sleeping. But when he took it into his warm kitchen, it uncurled promptly, stretched, and began to snap its teeth.

Groundhogs are plant eaters that feed during the day.

What happens to animals that die in the woods?

When animals die, they, like the leaves, twigs, and branches, decompose and turn back into soil. Some of the animals that die in the woods are killed by animals that need them as food. They disappear into various stomachs and are broken down there by enzymes. Other animals die of old age, because they are sick, or from some kind of accident. Fly maggots, fungi, and bacteria all help the decay of dead animals. Some small animals are not eaten, but they usually disappear just the same. They may be buried by the gravediggers of the woods, the sexton beetles. When these beetles find a dead baby bird, for example, they scurry all over it, almost seeming to take its measurements. Then they start to dig a hole. They work together, kicking dirt up out of the hole until it is deep enough. Then they run over to the body and crawl under it. Lying on their backs the beetles press their feet against the bird and heave. Little by little the body moves toward the hole, and at last drops into it. If the bird still sticks up a little too high, the beetles crawl down under it and dig some more. Then they kick dirt over the top until the bird has disappeared from sight. The entire operation generally takes several hours.

The sexton beetles don't do all this hard work just for the fun of it. They are really providing themselves with the right kind of place to lay their eggs. The female beetle lays them near the body, and when the tiny larvae hatch, they have plenty of rotten meat to eat. They grow and grow, and are called grubs, and when they are big enough, they become pupae. New sexton beetles hatch from the pupae, dig their way out of the ground, and fly off.

Sexton beetles

6 Projects to Do in the Forest

As you become familiar with the woods, the chances are that you will want to know by name more of its plants and animals. Getting to know the forest is something like being in a new class at school. On the first day all you notice is a sea of faces, and perhaps an old friend here or there. Then, little by little, each face starts to stand apart from the others, and soon you know everyone by name. After that, the names become more than names—they stand for individuals with distinct qualities. In the forest, as you get to know it, the same sort of thing happens, though it's a little harder to become as well acquainted. At first the trees are just a bunch of tree trunks. Then as you spend more time in the woods, you begin to see that the bark on one tree is different from the next, and so are the leaves, the arrangement of winter buds, and the way the limbs branch into twigs. At first you will remember only one or two names, and then as you begin to know what to look for, more and more trees will look like old friends.

A sunlit deciduous forest in early summer

This project section is designed to help you sharpen your powers of observation, so that you can begin to see qualities that distinguish one small flowering plant from another, one fern from the next, some of the fungi, the mosses, and so on. It gives you a number of different ways to preserve plants, so that later you can look up their names in identification manuals or take notes on what you have observed about them.

THE CANOPY

As we have already mentioned earlier in the book, you have to be something of a detective to explore the canopy. Few people except for scientists have the chance to observe life in the tops of the tall trees. But lots of evidence of life in the canopy falls from the trees to the forest floor, and you can learn a lot about the top layer of the forest from what you find below.

Leaves are the most obvious part of life in the canopy. One of the first things you can observe is the different patterns that the leaves make against the sky. If you are good with a camera, you can take pictures of these patterns.

Dead leaves fall to the forest floor, and living leaves are sometimes blown down during storms. Sometimes you find seedling trees growing beneath their parents. If you decide to learn the names of the many forest trees, studying leaves is a good way to do it. First of all, you need to keep some sort of record of the leaves you find. This can be done in a number of different ways.

If you are unable to get any deciduous leaves growing on the parent tree, try to find a seedling tree of the same variety. Gently bend the little tree over and lay its leaves down on a piece of drawing paper. You can use single sheets of paper fastened to a clipboard or to a piece of stiff cardboard, or you can bring a whole drawing pad to the woods. Choose a pencil with soft lead, for it will make a darker, more pleasing mark on the paper. A crayon that has been sharpened to a nice point would work well, too. Trace around the young leaf on the paper, and then draw a picture of the way the entire seedling looks. You might make a note of where you found the tree, such as in a sunny place, near rocks, and so on.

Perhaps you will manage to gather the leaves from a number of different deciduous trees, and instead of tracing them, you would like to press them. The best way to bring them home from the woods is in separate plastic bags. Make sure that you place the leaves flat inside the bags, so that they don't get crushed and bent. Once you have them home, you can look them up in a leaf-identification book, or you can press them first and later look up their names.

The easiest way to press a leaf is between sheets of newspaper, weighted down with a pile of heavy books. The most important thing to remember is to keep changing the layers of newspaper, so that the leaf gets drier and drier. The paper will become wet from the juices in the leaf, and the leaf will get moldy if you don't change the paper. Be careful, too, that the books don't get wet! Once the leaf is dry, glue it down on some stiff drawing paper or on a lightweight cardboard such as oaktag. Use a mixture of half glue—a white glue such as Elmer's works well—and half vinegar. There is an easy way to glue a leaf to paper. Spread the glue first on a sheet of glass or a piece of formica and lay the leaf down in the glue, pressing gently. Then pick up the leaf and lay it down carefully on the drawing paper or oaktag, again pressing gently. Do not move the leaf once it touches the paper. If you like, you can write your observations about the leaf on the sheet of paper.

Pressing leaves under books

newspaper

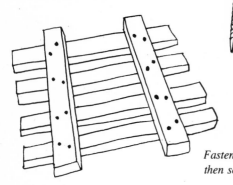

Fasten with glue,
then screws or nails.

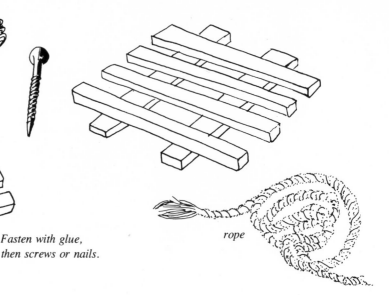

rope

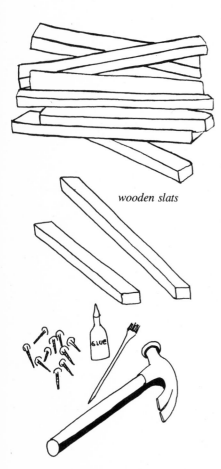

wooden slats

A well-pressed leaf is very flat, greenish, easy to glue, and easy to identify. If you save a leaf and do not press it, you will find that it curls up, wrinkles, and turns brown, and if you try to flatten it out, it crumbles. A curled, dried-up leaf can't be identified, for it looks quite different from the way it did on the tree. A pressed leaf will last for years and years if it is carefully handled.

If you have many different leaves that you would like to preserve, you may run out of heavy books to lay on top of them. Then it is time to build a leaf press.

To do this you will need eight or ten wooden slats about 1 or 2 inches wide. Fasten them together with crosspieces of the same size as the slats, so that they form two rectangles like those shown, each about 15 inches wide by 18 inches long. Cut five or six pieces of cardboard to the same size as the wooden frames.

To use the plant press, first place one wooden frame with the

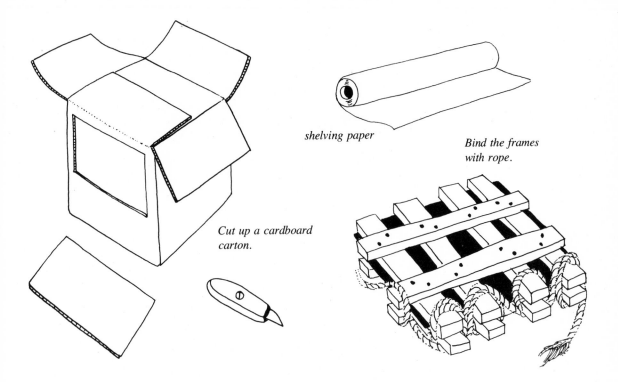

shelving paper

Cut up a cardboard carton.

Bind the frames with rope.

crosspieces facing down and the slats facing up. Then place a piece of cardboard on top of the frame. Next add a few sheets of newspaper and a piece of unwaxed shelving paper or blotting paper. Then place some of your leaves on the paper and cover them with another sheet of shelving or blotting paper. Add some more newspaper and another piece of cardboard. Keep on in this way, until you have several layers of leaves, separated by cardboard and newspaper. Then lay the second wooden frame on top, with the crosspieces facing up and the slats facing down. Bind the two frames together with rope. Every few days open your plant press and change the newspaper, for it will become damp. After a while your leaves will be very dry and flat.

By looking into tree and wild flower identification books, and by asking people who know something about flowers, trees, and other plants, you will probably be able to learn the names of most of the pressed specimens that you collect.

Sometimes you may want to do something else with the leaves you collect. If you like, you can pin a leaf to a piece of paper that has been fastened to a board. Then you can trace the outline of the leaf with a pencil, with a paintbrush and paint, or with splatter paint. When you unpin the leaf and lift it up, you will find you have made an outline or silhouette of its shape. A good tool to splatter paint with is an old toothbrush. You simply dip the toothbrush into some tempera paint and then draw the edge of a knife across the toothbrush toward yourself. Be sure you have the brush pointing toward your paper. It might be best to practice a little on newspaper before you start splattering your leaf.

Another thing you can do with a fresh leaf is ink it up with a water-base printing ink on a roller. (You can buy printing ink at an art supply store.) For this project you need a small pane of glass—tape the edges, so they can't cut you—a linoleum brayer or roller, and some printing ink and paper. Spread a small amount of ink evenly on the sheet of glass. Roll the brayer in the ink, put your leaf on a piece of newspaper, and roll the brayer over it. Then pick up your leaf and place it on a clean piece of newspaper, inky side up. Press a sheet of paper down on the leaf. When you take the paper off, you will have a print of the leaf.

Perhaps you would like to make a design from a number of leaf shapes. To do this, place a smooth piece of paper over a leaf, and with the flat bare side of a crayon, rub until you have an image of the leaf. If you put the leaf down with its veiny side up, you will have a more interesting rubbing than if you put it down with its smooth side up. When you have a number of rub-bings, you can cut them out and glue them down together on

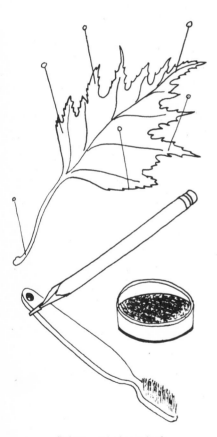

Splatter-painting a leaf

Inking leaves

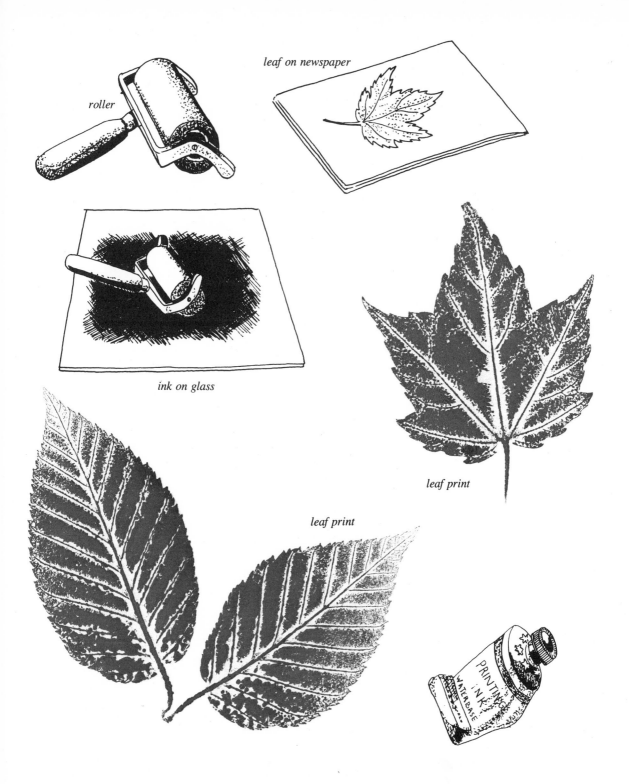

roller

leaf on newspaper

ink on glass

leaf print

leaf print

PRINTING INK WATERBASE

Crayon rubbings

another piece of paper, perhaps a piece of colored construction paper.

It is not too hard to learn how to make blueprints of pressed leaves, or if they are small enough, of complete plants you have pressed. Blueprint paper is specially treated so that it is sensitive to light and is available at architectural material supply houses and firms that make blueprints (check the yellow pages of your telephone directory).

First you must build yourself a blueprint frame. To do this you will need a piece of glass, about 5 inches by 7 inches, and a piece of cardboard cut to the same size. Tape the edges of the glass neatly so they are safe, and fasten one edge of the card-board to one edge of the glass. Buy some blueprint paper that is the same size as the frame you just made. Be sure to keep it in its lightproof envelop until you are ready to use it.

Wait for a sunny day; then put a leaf on the piece of glass and lay one sheet of the blueprint paper on top of the leaf, sensitive side down. Next lay the cardboard on top of the paper. Hold the glass tight against yourself and take the frame outside. Then turn it over so that sunlight can shine on the glass. You will be able to see your leaf, and the part of the blueprint paper that the leaf doesn't hide. To know how long you should leave the frame in the sun, you will have to experiment. The length of time varies from day to day and from season to season, depending on how intense the light from the sun is. Use your leaf and a test piece of blueprint paper, letting the sun shine on different parts of it for different amounts of time. When you think the paper has been exposed long enough, take it out of the frame and wash it in cold water. When the paper dries, you will have a blueprint of your leaf.

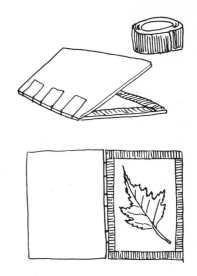

From pressed leaves you can make a card game very similar to the game called Authors. You will need four or five specimens of five different kinds of leaves—maple leaves, oak leaves, elm leaves, sassafras leaves, birch leaves—whatever varieties you can find. After they are well pressed and dry, glue the leaves down on small rectangles of oaktag. Then melt some paraffin wax on the stove. Never heat the wax directly over the flame. Always set the can with the wax in it in a pan of hot water, or in the top section of a double boiler. With a brush, paint a few thin layers of paraffin over the cards to protect the leaves.

Making a blueprint frame

To play the game, shuffle the cards and divide them between the players. The number of players depends on the number of sets of cards you have made. There must be one set for each person in the game and at least one extra set. Each player decides on the kind of leaves he or she wants to collect, but he must have at least two of that kind of leaf card in his hand to start to collect. Then, in turn, each player asks of another, "Do you have any maple leaves," or whatever kind of leaf he has decided to collect. The player that is asked must give up the

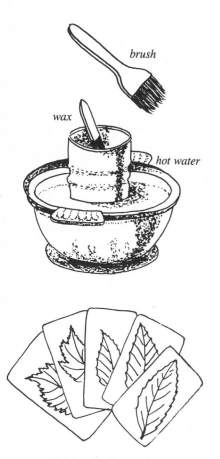

Making playing cards

card if he has it. And the person who asks must give a card, a "discard," to the player from whom he took the card. If the player who is asked does not have the card, play continues, with the next player asking the person on his right for such and such a card. Whenever a set is completed, the player puts it down in front of him, and the first one to have no cards left wins. This is a good project to do in the fall when the leaves are beautiful colors.

In all these projects you have been thinking mostly about the shapes of the leaves and the names of the trees from which they came. But you can look at leaves from a different point of view. Some of the leaves that you come across will have strange lumps, spots, or holes on them. See if you can find any that have been "mined" by leaf miners or that have been turned into galls. Some leaf galls fall to the forest floor. You might want to collect different kinds of leaf galls and look inside them to see if you can find out what organism is making them. If you can find a number of leaves from different trees that are still attached to twigs, compare the places where they are attached—the pulvinus area. Is it very different on different trees? You might also want to make a collection of twigs, and look them up in identification books to see if you can discover from which trees they have dropped. Winter is a good time to do this, for twigs have winter buds on them that are clues to naming the tree they come from. You can find books on twig identification in your local library and in bookstores in natural history museums.

Not all people are aware that many trees produce lovely flowers in the spring. Each tree has its own particular kind of flower, so this is another good way to become more familiar with the different kinds of trees. The tree flowers when they are

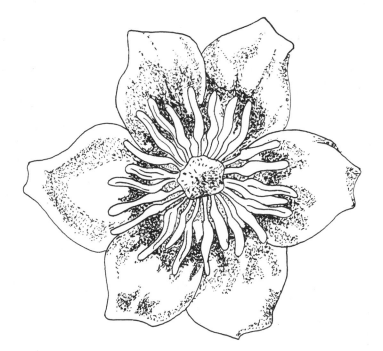

Tulip-tree flower

Norway maple twig

fertilized will develop seeds, so that you can also make a project of learning which trees make what kind of seed. For example, you may quickly learn to tell oak trees from other trees, but the next step is to learn to tell one kind of oak from another. Each kind makes a slightly different acorn. In the summer you can find them developing on the twigs, and in the fall you can find them on the ground.

Collect some needles from different kinds of conifers, and examine them carefully. Count how many needles there are in each bunch and observe how long they are and what shape they are. To find out what kind of tree they come from, look them up in an identification manual. In a coniferous forest you may be able to find some cones that the trees have dropped. Or perhaps

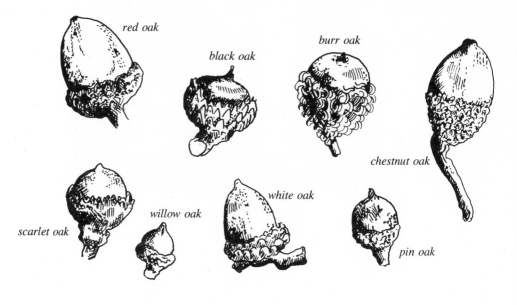

Different kinds of acorns

you will be able to observe or gather a green cone from the tree. Cones are another way to identify conifers, for each species of trees makes a different-shaped cone. As you begin to be able to tell one conifer from another, scout around to see if you can find a balsam tree. If you spot one, gather some dry needles from the ground beneath it and use them to make a balsam pillow. Or perhaps you can take some green needles from the tree and dry them yourself at home by spreading them out on newspaper or in a cardboard box.

If on a hot summer day you hear a terrific buzzing coming from the treetops, it is probably the sound of newly hatched cicadas. Check the trunks of the trees around you to see if you can find any of the empty cases that the cicadas climbed out of as they changed from nymph to adult. You might even find a live cicada ready to emerge, and it is a wonderful, very beautiful thing to watch.

THE MIDDLE LAYERS

The middle layers of the forest also offers a plentiful supply of leaves to study, but the middle layers in some of the more open forests may offer other rewards, too, for it is here that such shrubs as blackberries, blueberries, and raspberries grow, as well as the spicebush, the grapevine, and the honeysuckle vine. If you study well and learn your plants, you will soon know just which berries you can eat. You may also learn enough so that you will know which berries to pick for making jam and which are the right kind of sticks for weaving baskets and making Indian bows (the viburnums).

In the middle layers you can learn to distinguish trees in another way—by examining their bark. Each tree has its own kind of bark. One way to make a record of the patterns of bark is to lay a tough piece of paper against a tree and with the side of a peeled crayon rub over the surface of the paper. The rubbing will make the pattern clear and easy to identify. There are some pictures in this book of different bark patterns.

Sometimes you will find trees with bracket fungi growing on their trunks. You might make sketches of these on your pad, and take them home to look up. Make a note of the type of tree the fungi were growing on if you know.

If you find a dead tree in the woods, peel away some of the bark and see if there are tunnels underneath it. See if you can find any insects or worms or grubs living under the bark.

If you find a tent caterpillar's nest, come back several days in a row to see what progress the creatures are making in devouring the leaves of the tree. If you can, check the nest early in the morning and at night to see what the animals are doing at those times.

Honeysuckle

You may be able to find a rocky outcropping in the woods. Make a note of the kinds of plants you find in the wet places and in the dry ones. See if any small trees are growing out of cracks in the rock, and try to find out what kinds they are.

THE GROUND COVER

As you explore the ground cover, you may feel a little overwhelmed by the number of different kinds of small plants there are. And you may feel that you want to collect some to take home to press and identify. Before you do so, it's a good idea to write to the botany department of your state university for a list of the rare flowers in your area that should never be picked. A

Bluets (left), *Houstonia caerulia,* and spring beauties, *Claytonia virginica.* Both plants are found in deciduous woods in early spring.

Violets (left), which come in many different varieties in the woods, and an Indian cucumber

good rule of thumb to follow is this: if you can't see at least a dozen of the same kind of plant growing within view, don't pick the lonely flower. Unless you are really serious about doing something with a plant—unless you must pick it to make a detailed drawing or for identification purposes—it is better to leave it in the woods.

One tip on collecting whole plants—if you take along a single paper or a plastic bag, all your specimens may get jumbled together and ruined. A magazine works much better. Each different plant can be carefully laid on a different page of the magazine, and you can keep notes on where you found it in the margins of the page. You might want to write down whether you found it in a coniferous or in a broadleaf forest, in an open space or in the shade, and so on.

Leaves are easy to arrange neatly inside a press, because they are small and generally flat. It is a little harder to arrange a complete plant with all its leaves and possibly a flower. If the plant is too long to fit in the press, you must cut it into two sections, or better yet, bend it into a Z shape. Try and spread the leaves apart enough so that when they are dry you will be able to see their shapes.

Ferns are probably one of the most beautiful of the plants of the ground cover to try and get to know, and to identify a fern you need take only one frond home.

If you find a valley of violets, you might take a few flowers both to look at and to study. Look far down under the leaves and see if you can find any of the cleistogamous buds. Take one of the flowers apart and see if you can recognize all the different parts.

Many of the beautiful spring wild flowers are becoming quite rare and need to be protected. It is better to let them be, and to

Birds-foot violet

bring paper and pencil and perhaps try to draw them, making notes about where you found them.

Wild strawberry

On still another trip to the woods you might look for tiny mosses, trees, and other plants for a terrarium. A big pickle jar, turned on its side, or a large fish tank make good containers to hold a woodland scene that you can put together yourself. If you use the jar, you will need to build a small rack from slats to hold the jar and keep it from rolling. It is a good idea to start any terrarium with a layer of small stones or gravel topped by a couple of inches of sand. These layers create drainage, and keep the soil in the terrarium from becoming mucky. On top of the sand put a layer of forest soil. Then you are ready to add your plants.

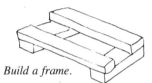

Build a frame.

Make sure you collect each tiny tree or fern or other plant with all its roots and a little extra dirt. An acorn in your terrarium will sprout into a tiny oak, and the seedlings from other broad-leaved and needle-leaved trees will do very well in your miniature forest. Wrap each plant, after you dig it up, in a piece of newspaper, so that it won't get injured on the way home. There are lots of plants to choose from besides tree seedlings and ferns—partridge berries, wintergreen, violets, club mosses, wild strawberries, and so on. And if you know how to feed it, you might even put a toad, a frog, or a red eft into your terrarium.

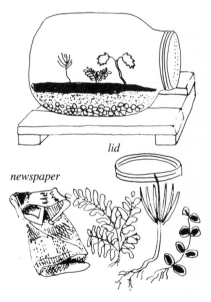

lid

newspaper

Making a terrarium

When you have planted everything, cover the top with a piece of glass, leaving a small space between the tank and the glass so that air can get in. If you are using a pickle jar, you can make small holes in the lid before screwing on the lid. Once it is made, a terrarium needs watering only once in a while. It is good not to get it too wet, but if you do, simply leave off the lid for a while, and the soil will dry out. When you make a terrarium, you are re-creating the beauty you found in the woods, and having it inside, you can enjoy it all year long.

You can study the habits of certain live insects right in the woods. If you watch carefully, you can see what business an ant is about. Or you can delve into the foam of the spittlebug to see if you can find out what the creature looks like who makes so much spit.

You can study live insects at home, also. If you make a small cage for a cricket or grasshopper, you can keep it as a pet for a long time, feeding it bits of fruit, salad greens, and sometimes meat. Or you can keep caterpillars in a cage or jar, feeding them leaves from the plant where you found them, and watch them spin cocoons or make chrysalises, and finally turn into moths and butterflies. Be sure to provide a stick for the caterpillar inside the cage or jar, and leave plenty of room for the wings to open downward. After the insect emerges, either set it loose or kill it and mount it as described below.

Many people like to make permanent collections of the insects they find. Some insects you can capture by hand, and some you must catch in a net.

To make a net, take a fairly stiff piece of wire and shape it into a loop. Twist the two ends of the wire together where they meet to form a small handle that can be tied to a stick for extra length and strength. Then sew a long bag, using a piece of cheesecloth, old curtain material—the kind that looks like netting—or an old stocking. Make the net twice as long as the diameter of the opening. Use heavy thread to sew the net onto the wire loop.

After you have caught an insect, you must kill it, if you want

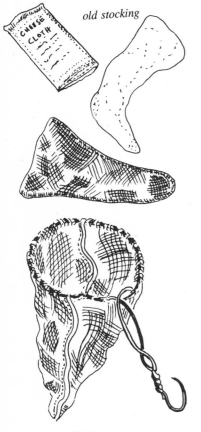

old stocking

Making a net

to make it part of a permanent collection. So you need an in-sect-killing jar. A wide-mouthed, pint-sized Mason jar works well. Either you can put some nail-polish remover onto a piece of cotton and hide the cotton in the bottom of the jar behind a piece of cardboard, or you can mix up a little plaster of Paris, pour it in the bottom of the jar, and when the plaster has dried, pour a little nail-polish remover onto it. Keep the jar tightly covered and do not breathe the fumes. Drop the insects you catch into the jar and replace the lid. Once your insects are dead, you can store them in shoe or cigar boxes that have been lined with cardboard and white shelving paper. Stick a pin right through the insect into the cardboard bottom of the box. If the insects have thick bodies, place a mothball in the box with them. It will help preserve them.

shoebox

cardboard

killing jar

water

dry plaster

mothball

Killing and storing insects

THE SOIL

In order to get a feeling for the layers of soil in the forest, it is best to go out with a shovel and dig down a way into the earth. Then you can look over the layers carefully, noticing the changes in color from one to the other.

You may be able to see some soil organisms creeping and climbing through the litter—a world of leaves and sticks, crumbling wood and plant stems. Perhaps you will begin to notice worm holes, and see the castings that earthworms leave at the entrances to their tunnels.

You will, no doubt, be able to find leaves in various stages of decay, and rotting logs with rhizomorphs running through them. You may be able to spot a slime mold, and without question you will begin to notice many different kinds and colors of mushrooms.

Mushrooms (the silky Volvaria) growing on the side of a tree

tin can with water

corn-starch

plaster

the cast

Casting a footprint

If you own or can borrow a book about identifying mushrooms, take it into the forest with you, for that is the best place to begin to know the fungi. They are hard to bring home in one piece, and in any case, some of them are poisonous, so it's better to leave them where they are.

On another walk in the woods, take along a little sack of plaster of Paris, some cornstarch, a coffee can (or some other container with a wide opening and a lid) filled with water, and a bunch of 3-inch-wide strips of thin cardboard. On this visit search carefully for sharp, clear animal tracks. You are most likely to find animal footprints in damp places in the forest.

When you find a footprint, make a little wall around it with the strips of cardboard, and then sprinkle a thin layer of cornstarch over the track. Next mix the plaster with the water. It will help if you have already practiced doing this at home, so you will know exactly how to do it. (Plaster of Paris is best mixed by sprinkling it into the container of water until it forms a little island of dry plaster; then stir the water and plaster together.) When you have mixed a nice batch of thick creamy plaster, pour it into the animal track and wait for it to harden. This takes about twenty minutes, and the plaster will first grow hot, then cool as it stiffens. When it is hard, lift it out of the animal track and clean it off. You will have an exact replica of the bottom of an animal's foot.

This same project can be done at home, with some leaves or nuts or seeds or twigs that you have brought home from the woods. Roll out a smooth layer of plastelene (an oil clay you can buy at stores with an art-supply counter). Then lay your specimen on top of it. Take a rolling pin and press the leaf, or what have you, into the plastelene. Then remove the leaf. You will have made an imprint in the clay. Build a small wall around the imprint as you did around the track in the woods, and cast the imprint in plaster.

Now you have explored the forest from the canopy to the soil, and have begun to be familiar with the members of this thriving community. As you get to know the forest better and better, you will find that its beauty enriches your life in many ways.

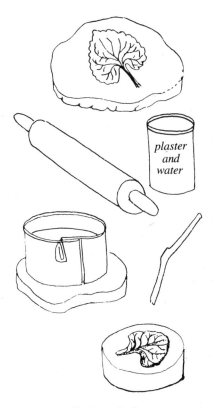

plaster and water

Casting a leaf

Actual Sizes of Animals and Plants

Following are the approximate actual lengths of the animals illustrated throughout the book. The drawings of plants and of parts of plants vary from one quarter of actual size to actual size.

Bibliography

BASIC TEXTS AND REFERENCE WORKS

Allee, Warder, C., et. al. *Principles of Animal Ecology*. Philadelphia: W. B. Saunders Company, 1949.

Benton, Allen H., and Werner, William E., Jr. *Field Biology and Ecology*. New York: McGraw-Hill Book Company, 1974.

Buchsbaum, Ralph, and Buchsbaum, Mildred. *Basic Ecology*. Pittsburgh: Boxwood Press, 1957.

Elton, Charles S. *The Ecology of Animals*. New York: John Wiley and Sons, 1953.

Kendeigh, Charles S. *Animal Ecology*. Englewood Cliffs, N.J.: Prentice-Hall, 1961.

Milne, Lorus, and Milne, Margery. *The Balance of Nature*. New York: Alfred A. Knopf, 1960.

Neal, Ernest. *Woodland Ecology*. Cambridge: Harvard University Press, 1960.

Odum, Eugene P., and Odum, Howard T. *Fundamentals of Ecology*. Philadelphia: W. B. Saunders Company, 1959.

Richards, Paul W. *The Tropical Rain Forest*. New York: Cambridge University Press, 1952.

Russell, John E. *The World of the Soil*. London: Collins, 1957.

Shelford, Victor E. *The Ecology of North America*. Urbana: University of Illinois Press, 1963.

Spurr, Stephen. *Forest Ecology*. New York: Ronald Press Company, 1964.

Storer, John H. *The Web of Life*. Old Greenwich, Conn.: Devin-Adair, 1960.

FIELD GUIDES AND HOW-TO-DO-IT BOOKS

Bigelow, Howard E. *The Mushroom Pocket Field Guide*. New York: Macmillan Publishing Company, 1974. (Fine guide in full color. It really fits in the pocket!)

Birdseye, Clarence, and Birdseye, Eleanor. *Growing Woodland*

Plants. New York: Dover Publications, 1972. (Information on which forest plants you can grow and how to do it.)

Blakeslee, Albert F., and Jarvis, Chester D. *Northeastern Trees in Winter*. New York: Dover Publications, 1972.

Bland, John H. *Forests of Lilliput: The Realm of Mosses and Lichens*. Englewood Cliffs, N.J.: Prentice-Hall, 1971. (A fascinating book about the lore and science of mosses and lichens.)

Cobb, Boughton. *Field Guide to the Ferns*. Boston, Houghton Mifflin Company, 1963.

Collingwood, G. H., and Brush, Warren D. *Knowing Your Trees*. Washington, D.C.: American Forestry Assoc., 1964.

Comstock, Anna Botsford. *Handbook of Nature Study*. Ithaca, N.Y.: Comstock Publishing Associates, a division of Cornell University Press, 1961. (A one-of-a-kind, classic nature-study book.)

Conard, Henry S. *How to Know the Mosses and Liverworts*. Dubuque, Iowa: William C. Brown Company, 1956. (An inexpensive guide.)

Farb, Peter. *Ecology*. New York: Time-Life Books, a division of Time Inc., 1963.

Hillcourt, William. *The New Field Book of Nature Activities and Hobbies*. New York: G. P. Putnam's Sons, 1970. (Includes a section on trees, and many other useful chapters.)

Krieger, Louis C. *The Mushroom Handbook*. New York: Dover Publications, 1967. (A well-illustrated guide to the common mushrooms in the eastern United States.)

McCormick, Jack. *The Life of the Forest*. New York: McGraw-Hill Book Company, 1966.

McMinn, Howard E., and Maino, Evelyn. *An Illustrated Manual of Pacific Coast Trees*. Berkeley: University of California Press, 1946.

Morgan, Ann H. *Field Book of Animals in Winter*. New York: G. P. Putnam's Sons, 1939.

Murie, Olaus J. *A Field Guide to Animal Tracks*. Boston: Houghton Mifflin Company, 1954.

Palmer, Ralph S. *The Mammal Guide*. New York: Doubleday and Company, 1954.

Peattie, Donald C. *A Natural History of Western Trees,* Boston: Houghton Mifflin Company, 1953.

Peterson, Roger Tory. *A Field Guide to the Birds*. Boston: Houghton Mifflin Company, 1947.

————. *A Field Guide to Western Birds*. Boston: Houghton Mifflin Company, 1961.

Petrides, George A. *A Field Guide to Trees and Shrubs*. Boston: Houghton Mifflin Company, 1958. (Guide to trees, shrubs, and woody vines in the northeastern and north central United States. An easy-to-use book.)

Platt, Rutherford. *The Great American Forest*. Englewood Cliffs, N.J.: Prentice-Hall, Inc., 1971. (A hymn of praise to the forests, but with facts to back it up. One of the books that truly conveys the aesthetic values of a forest.)

Sargent, Charles S. *Manual of Trees of North America*. New York: Dover Publications, 1961. (A classic!)

Smith, Alexander H. *The Mushroom Hunter's Field Guide*. Ann Arbor: University of Michigan Press, 1963. (One of the best guides, with abundant black-and-white photos of each mushroom.)

————. *A Field Guide to the Western Mushrooms*. Ann Arbor: University of Michigan Press. 1975. (The western counterpart to the above book.)

Stupka, Arthur. *Trees, Shrubs, and Woody Vines of the Great Smoky Mountains National Park*. Knoxville: University of Tennessee Press, 1964.

Sudworth, George B. *Forest Trees of the Pacific Slope*. New York: Dover Publications, 1967. (Beautiful drawings and descriptions; a useful book.)

Swain, Ralph B. *The Insect Guide*. New York: Doubleday and Company, 1948.

Symonds, G. W. *The Shrub Identification Book*. New York: William Morrow and Company, 1963.

————. *The Tree Identification Book*. New York: William Morrow and Company, 1963. (Both these books are useful pictorial guides to the identification of many hundreds of shrubs and trees in the northeastern United States.)

Wherry, Edgar, T. *Wild Flower Guide*. New York: Doubleday and Company, 1948.

Index

(Page numbers in italics indicate photographs.)

ABOUT THE AUTHORS

Albert List, Jr., was graduated from Cornell University, where he conducted detailed studies of the honey locust tree and the structure of roots and where in 1958 he received his M.S. degree in botany and in 1961 his Ph.D. An associate professor at Drexel University, he is currently engaged in research on soil organisms in the White Mountains of New Hampshire and plant growth. The author of numerous articles for scientific journals, Professor List spends as much of his spare time as he can in the forest, hiking, canoeing, and mountain climbing.

Ilka List was graduated from the University of Maine, where she received a degree in art education. She has studied botany and marine zoology at St. Andrews University in Scotland and biology, literature, and philosophy at Cornell University, Reed College, and Upsala College. An art teacher for a number of years, Ms. List is the author of three children's books. She lives with her family on a farm in the state of New York, where she raises goats and horses and devotes as much time as she can to her work as a sculptor.